design YOUR OWN furniture

from concept to completion

JIM STACK

POPULAR WOODWORKING BOOKS
CINCINNATI, OHIO
www.popularwoodworking.com

Design Your Own Furniture. Copyright © 2002 by Jim Stack. Manufactured in Singapore. All rights reserved. No part of this book may be reproduced in any form or by any electronic or mechanical means, including information storage and retrieval systems, without permission in writing from the publisher, except by a reviewer, who may quote brief passages in a review. Published by Popular Woodworking Books, an imprint of F&W Publications, Inc., 4700 E. Galbraith Road, Cincinnati, Ohio, 45236. First edition.

Visit our Web site at www.popularwoodworking.com for more information and resources for woodworkers.

Other fine Popular Woodworking Books are available from your local bookstore or direct from the publisher.

06   05   04   03   02   5   4   3   2   1

Library of Congress Cataloging-in-Publication Data
Stack, Jim, 1951-
    Design your own furniture / by Jim Stack.-- 1st ed.
      p.
    Includes index.
    ISBN 1-55870-613-5 (pbk: alk. paper)
    ISBN 1-55870-655-0 (pob: alk. paper)
    1. Furniture making--Amateurs' manuals. I. Title.

TT195 .S673 2002
684.1'04--dc21
2002068442

Edited by Jennifer Ziegler
Designed by Brian Roeth
Production coordinated by Mark Griffin
Technical Illustrations drawn by Jim Stack

READ THIS IMPORTANT SAFETY NOTICE

To prevent accidents, keep safety in mind while you work. Use the safety guards installed on power equipment; they are for your protection. When working on power equipment, keep fingers away from saw blades, wear safety goggles to prevent injuries from flying wood chips and sawdust, wear headphones to protect your hearing and consider installing a dust vacuum to reduce the amount of airborne sawdust in your woodshop. Don't wear loose clothing, such as neckties or shirts with loose sleeves, or jewelry, such as rings, necklaces or bracelets, when working on power equipment. Tie back long hair to prevent it from getting caught in your equipment. People who are sensitive to certain chemicals should check the chemical content of any product before using it. The authors and editors who compiled this book have tried to make the contents as accurate and correct as possible. Plans, illustrations, photographs and text have been carefully checked. All instructions, plans and projects should be carefully read, studied and understood before beginning construction. Due to the variability of local conditions, construction materials, skill levels, etc., neither the author nor Popular Woodworking Books assumes any responsibility for any accidents, injuries, damages or other losses incurred resulting from the material presented in this book. Prices listed for supplies and equipment were current at the time of publication and are subject to change. Glass shelving should have all edges polished and must be tempered. Untempered glass shelves may shatter and can cause serious bodily injury. Tempered shelves are very strong and if they break will just crumble, minimizing personal injury.

METRIC CONVERSION CHART

to convert	to	multiply by
Inches	Centimeters	2.54
Centimeters	Inches	0.4
Feet	Centimeters	30.5
Centimeters	Feet	0.03
Yards	Meters	0.9
Meters	Yards	1.1
Sq. Inches	Sq. Centimeters	6.45
Sq. Centimeters	Sq. Inches	0.16
Sq. Feet	Sq. Meters	0.09
Sq. Meters	Sq. Feet	10.8
Sq. Yards	Sq. Meters	0.8
Sq. Meters	Sq. Yards	1.2
Pounds	Kilograms	0.45
Kilograms	Pounds	2.2
Ounces	Grams	28.4
Grams	Ounces	0.035

DEDICATION

about the author

By formal education, Jim Stack is a musician, specifically a composer. He studied the great composers; analyzed style, harmony, melody, cultural influences, and drew upon these elements to form his own compositions. Making a living in music is a struggle and Jim found he was not well suited to the life of a musician. In the course of self-discovery he found he had a talent and a desire to be a woodworker.

Jim started out managing a furniture restoration shop and learned how to repair peeling wood veneer, reglue broken parts and refinish furniture. After moving to Cincinnati and working for fifteen years in furniture- and cabinet-making shops, Jim opened his own woodworking shop. He then spent five and a half years designing and building custom cabinets and furniture.

Jim now enjoys teaching others the joy and satisfaction that come with working with your hands to create cabinetry and furniture.

acknowledgements

I owe much to all the furniture designers and makers whom I have known and worked with over the years. Each one taught me specific techniques that are needed to design and build furniture. I appreciate the sharing of their knowledge, patience when I became frustrated and encouragement to try new things. I learned not to be afraid of trying different ways to design and build furniture.

special thanks

I want to give special thanks to the folks at *Popular Woodworking* magazine. Publisher Steve Shanesy, senior editors David Thiel and Chris Schwarz, former editor Jim Stuard and contributors Troy Sexton and Glen Huey are some of the best craftsmen I've ever worked with, and their work is shown throughout this book.

I've used several photos of Rick Williams's furniture designs, also. He is the best furniture-making carpenter I've ever met!

I also borrowed a photo of a computer desk designed by my father, Ken Stack. He is 80 years young and has been building furniture and cabinets as a hobby for at least 51 years.

To designer Brian Roeth and my editor Jenny Ziegler, I give you thanks for all your encouragement and great work on this book.

TABLE *of*
contents

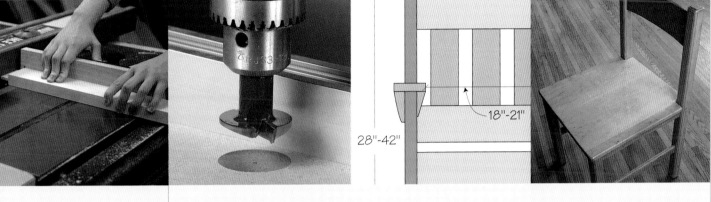

INTRODUCTION *to*
designing furniture

This book is for you, the furniture and cabinetmakers who like to create with your minds and hands.

I hope it will help you learn the language of designing and building. After you've learned this language, you'll have your own voice and can start saying what it is you want to say.

I've included lots of photos of different styles and shapes of furniture and cabinets. It's easier to show you a photo and explain what I'm talking about than use lots of words to describe things.

I offer some questions and answers about designing and building, some dos and don'ts, and some advice and tips. I want to encourage you to experience the joy of using the creative process to take a journey into the world of three- and four-dimensional thinking. Make it a good journey with lots of sight-seeing and learning.

I'd like to remind you to keep it simple, with a touch of elegance, and try to create a good, relaxed feeling with the furniture you design and build.

Learn how a piece of furniture is put together. What joinery can be used? What kind of woods or other materials can be used? What is the function of the piece? How is it finished? What is the style? Each of these elements is important and should be considered when designing furniture.

Many times, when you have a great idea, you want to start building it as soon as possible. You jump in too soon, start making mistakes and the spirit of the project is lost. Begin with the end in mind and remember that how you do something is at least as important as what you are doing, so do your best and enjoy the journey.

chapter **1**

design
elements

What are the **ingredients** of good furniture design, and what makes

one **style** different from another? How can you use these **design**

elements to build furniture for your home?

The wardrobe above is a contemporary piece that has an Art Deco-influenced style. The sideboard on page 8 is in the Arts & Crafts style. Both pieces have straight lines, drawers with flat faces and use the wood grains to create beautiful patterns. What are the differences between these two pieces, and what are the similarities? What makes these two different styles work individually?

deas are usually born out of much research and observation of things around us. Inspiration for furniture designs can be found everywhere. Of course, we can start with woodworking books and magazines which are filled with hundreds of projects, tips, tricks and new methods of working. But don't stop there.

The mall is also a great place for ideas. Yes, the mall! Many stores have the latest fads and ideas for just about everything, including furniture. Display cabinets for jewelry or clothes can give you a new idea for building a set of shelves for the bedroom. The mall storefronts are usually built with well-thought-out mouldings, trim and fasteners.

Another place to find furniture inspiration is television. I've seen some great furniture on the sets of sitcoms and dramas. And the sets of news broadcasts can be very clever, offering unique ideas for the shape of a desk or chair.

Magazines, especially those created for the homeowner, offer an almost infinite variety of furniture, cabinet and room designs. Be sure to look at the advertisements in magazines. Some will contain a room setting that is totally unique, from the placement of the furniture to the style and cabinetry.

Creating something unique is a tough job because it seems like it's all been done before. What amazes me is how new designs are constantly appearing using new methods of construction for chairs, tables and all the other pieces of furniture we build.

the ELEMENTS *of* DESIGN

construction materials

For most furniture and cabinetmakers, the material of choice is wood. But that has changed over the years. New man-made solid-surface materials like Corian and other brands are used for counter-tops, bar fronts, walls, desktops, reception areas — the list is endless. These materials have proven themselves to be very durable and stylish, and the colors and patterns available are almost limitless. These materials can look exactly like mar-ble, granite, sandstone or any solid color of your choice. When finished, they can be worked to any sheen desired. If sanded with ultrafine sandpaper, a high-gloss finish can even be attained.

High-pressure laminates have been around since the late 1930s and are still used today. They also come in any pattern or color imaginable. These laminates are especially good when used as counter-tops. The durability is incredible. They can last for years and sometimes decades. Acid-resistant laminates are available for laboratories. Complete rooms have been made with laminates. They can cover walls, floors and now even the furniture.

But for most cabinetmakers and furni-ture builders, wood is still the most re-warding material to work with. As builders, we can use wood for its color, durability, flexibility and strength; but the wood itself always has the final say. The grain patterns are never the same, color is never consis-tent and it expands and contracts with changes in the weather. There is nothing that can be done about it; we work within the parameters that the wood sets.

I DEFINE DESIGN ELEMENTS AS all the things that determine what a piece of furniture will look like and how it will function. Ask yourself: What materials are used? What is the style, shape? How are the lines defined on the piece? Are there straight or curved lines on the legs or doors? Do the lines end abruptly, or do they flow into one another? Are there lots of carvings or mouldings on the piece?

When we set out to make a piece of furniture, we make a lot of choices un-consciously. Certain styles of furniture ap-peal to us, and we base our choices on those likes and dislikes.

When I was growing up in the 1950s, I remember seeing lots of furniture made of big, thick, heavy and very dark-colored wood. Most of it was old, tired and falling apart, and I thought, "This is not the kind of furniture that I would like to

have in my house!" As it turns out, years later I found out that it was Arts & Crafts furniture. It is now in a revival of sorts, and people love it. It is easy to build and very sturdy, and the materials are reason-ably priced. I've made some Arts & Crafts pieces that were fun to make and looked good, but in the back of my mind I still have that memory of when I first encoun-tered the style.

The design elements for Arts & Crafts furniture are predominantly straight lines, thick legs on chairs and tables, corbels (those bookshelf bracket-looking sup-ports), dark stained wood and quarter-sawn white oak.

Now think about Shaker-style furni-ture. What design elements tell you it's Shaker? It has straight lines, a few curved lines; some pieces are painted, and others are stained wood; the legs on tables are

Take that crown moulding motif a little farther by giving it a curve. Add some moulding on the face of the header while you're at it. This is a bookcase made of poplar that had me fooled. I thought it was cherry!

When we set out to make a piece of furniture,
we make a lot of choices unconsciously.

tapered (either square or turned); the woods are maple, pine, poplar, walnut, cherry and birch; it has frame-and-panel doors, but no ornamentation and the pieces generally have a visual lightness. A lot of the same elements make up both styles but they are very different!

Art Deco is a style that had worldwide appeal. Everyone had their own ideas of what the furniture should look like. Some basic design elements are common to this particular style: wood veneers, silver, stainless steel, ebonized maple, real ebony and exotic-wood veneer inlays. The designs incorporated a lot of curves and stained woods. The ebony and ebonized maple were used as decoration, as well as door and drawer hardware.

In the 1700s and 1800s, the United States received lots of immigrants who brought their customs, languages and woodworking skills with them. Boston, New York, Philadelphia and Baltimore were the major creative centers for furniture and cabinetmakers. Their skills were passed on to others and found their way into the countryside. The furniture became less decorated and more practical. The country cabinetmakers had clients with basic needs and little money, so their craft reflects this. The workmanship was good enough for many of these pieces to

Some very talented people in this world can do wonderful things with their hands and minds. This is a great example of how ornamentation can change the whole look and feel of a Queen Anne-style leg. The carving on the foot is not so uncommon, but the carving at the top of the leg is amazing. This leg is part of a large dining table that can have this type of adornment and not be overpowered by it.

thinking outside the box

One of the toughest things for a craftsman to do is design — I mean *just* design and not think about how the piece of furniture is going to be built, what kind of joinery will work the best, if the piece will actually stay together or how much the materials will cost.

Letting our minds be free to play with *just* form and function is tough. I have a brother-in-law who can do that. He has no problem visualizing forms, textures and function. Then when it comes to the execution of his ideas, I am able to help him work out the details of construction, but I do envy his ability to separate his free-thinking from his practical "how do we build this thing?" thinking.

survive for over 200 years!

When I am going to build a piece of furniture, whether it be a table, chair, dresser or kitchen cabinet, I always start from the beginning. If it is a table, I start with the basic concept of a table — four legs and a top. What happens after that is determined by several factors. Where is it going to be located? Is there anything else in the room that could or should be matched stylewise? Does the room have lots of natural light or is it fairly dark? Is it a small or large room? All these things help me determine what the table should look like.

If there are other pieces of furniture in

This is a country-style Queen Anne table. The unusual disks at the corners of the top offer extra space and a distinctive look. The legs are unadorned and are almost straight. These legs can be made fairly easily on a lathe, but they still have that strong Queen Anne flavor. The simple scrollwork on the aprons and the curly grained wood give this table a flair all its own.

This knockdown Arts & Crafts bookcase is made with removable wedges. This piece can be taken apart, moved and reassembled easily. Also, this wedged joint is strong and stable.

the room, are they all the same style or mixed styles? Let's say the style of the room is Early American with a touch of Queen Anne. I would probably decide to make a table with cabriole legs. Maybe I'd use some veneers on the aprons. Is the room naturally lit? If so, a darker wood could be used to make the table, possibly walnut or mahogany. If the room is darker, a better wood to use would be ash or maple. These lighter woods can then be stained to a medium color. The reason for using a lighter wood in a darker room is for feel. A dark table in a dimly lit room can appear large and awkward, whereas the lighter table will appear to be just that — lighter and friendlier.

Next is the size of the table. How large is the room? That will dictate what size the table will be.

What else needs to be determined? If it's a dining table, will it need leaves, and if so, how many?

Now is the time to start sketching. Every cabinetmaker and furniture maker I have ever worked with cannot talk without waving their hands around. They build things in the air by saying it's this long and that wide and it's shaped like this. What inevitably happens is pencils come out and we start drawing on whatever is available. Many a cabinet has been designed on a scrap piece of plywood, that was then cut up to make that very cabinet! It's important to start sketching whatever it is you will be making, as this will help you visualize the project.

HANDLES, KNOBS *and* HINGES

ONE OF THE MOST IMPORTANT decisions to make when building furniture is choosing the handles, knobs and hinges. As I will state elsewhere in this book, I always told my clients to wait until their furniture or cabinetry was finished before choosing the hardware. I once designed a cabinet around a set of handles a client had picked out. It was an interesting task, and I learned a lot about how hardware effects the final look, feel and function of a piece of furniture.

For example, Arts & Crafts furniture has its own hardware designs. The bail pulls, knobs, hinges and catches are cast metal. If you want to make your Arts & Crafts project look authentic, the choice is to go with this hardware.

The Shakers, likewise, designed knobs that have become famous. In the interest of speed and economy, the Shaker craftsmen turned their knobs on lathes. They could really crank these things out. After all, they were making furniture for an entire community and were selling them to other communities as well.

The purpose of handles and knobs is obvious, but it became part of the trademark of builders to make their own door and drawer pulls or to have them made to their specifications.

Most things get designed by trial and error. The Shakers wanted knobs that could be easily grasped, but they wanted them to be plain. They discovered that a mushroom-shaped knob was comfortable to the fingers, plain-looking, and that when the knobs were viewed from the front they became almost invisible.

An example of modern day trial and error occurs in some of the shops I've

This is a small turned knob set into a recess which has been carved with a gouge. This whimsical idea was done just for the fun of it, but it looked great when it was finished.

This is a handle on a file cabinet. I like the way it looks and feels. Handles made from materials that contrast with the cabinet can be very attractive.

This drawer pull is simply routed into the drawer front, and fingers fit comfortably into the cavities. This is a sleek look that requires a little finesse. You need a special router bit and confidence that you are placing the pull where you want it!

The yellow lines divide the
distance between the blue
center line to the outside
corners of the cabinet into
equal parts on both sides
of the cabinet.

The Greene brothers were U.S. designers and
builders who worked in the early 1900s. Their
pieces included Japanese design elements. The
stepback at the top of the front leg on this bench is
a good example of the subtle but effective design
elements they used.

The use of bookmatched veneers, black knobs, angles on the cabinet corners which would usually be
square, and the reddish stained cabinet sides all give this piece an Art Deco flavor.

worked in over the years. We would make
screw caddies that we could carry around
the shop so that we would have all the
screws we needed for assemblies right at
our side. It usually turned into a competi-
tion as to who could make the fanciest
or strangest-looking handles for these
caddies. I must say, it brought out the
creativity in us! We discovered things like,
if the handle on the caddy was too tall,
when the caddy was on the floor we
would always trip over the handles. This

would tip the caddy over, and we'd have
to sort out screws.

The placement of knobs is of the ut-
most importance. Some folks scoff at this
idea, but if asked where they would like
their knobs or handles placed, they all
have different opinions. On the dresser
above, I tried several different configurations of knob placement. I tried one handle in the middle of each drawer, but that
wasn't enough to balance the piece, and it
conflicted with the tapered sides. I tried

two knobs on each drawer, lined up vertically with one another. Again, this just
didn't look right. Then I came up with
the idea of lining up the knobs parallel to
the tapered sides, but that wasn't it either,
because the line of the knobs didn't work
with the center line of the cabinet. Finally
I realized that the sides had a vanishing
point somewhere above the top of the
cabinet, so I divided the bottom of the
cabinet into sections, then divided the
top into sections with the same proportions as the bottom. This was the right
way to attach the knobs for this cabinet,
and it really made the unit come alive!

Hinges are an interesting piece of
hardware. They make it possible to close
off the inside of a cabinet, yet also expose
that same interior. A very clever inven-

One of the most important decisions to be made when building furniture is choosing the handles, knobs and hinges.

These are European hinges and hardware. On the left, top to bottom, is a confirmat screw, a 5mm steel shelf pin, a 7mm shelf pin with a collar and a ¼" L-shaped shelf clip. In the center are hinges and plates. The brown plastic cylinder and screw, at the top of the photo, is a drawer-front adjuster. It is inserted into the drawer front and held on the drawer box with the screw. The screw is in an eccentric that allows up to ³⁄₁₆" movement of the drawer front in all directions.

By combining hinges and their plates, you can hang a full-overlay, half-overlay or inset door. The hinge plates come in heights of 0mm, 3mm, 6mm and 9mm. The hinges come in straight (middle hinge in photo), half cranked (top and bottom hinges) and full cranked. For example, if you used a straight hinge with a 0mm or 3mm plate, you would be hanging a full-overlay door. If you used a half-cranked hinge and a 0mm or 3mm plate, you would be hanging a half-overlay door. Combine a 6mm plate and a half-cranked hinge (top hinge and plate to its right), you would be hanging an inset door. For an inset door, you could also use a 0mm or 3mm plate and a full-cranked hinge. The hinge at the bottom of the photo will clip onto the plate to its right. This is very handy for moving cabinets after the doors have been hung and set. Simply remove the door and rehang it when the cabinet is in place.

tion! (Drawers are really clever, too, when you think about it.)

There are several ways to hang a door — by its right or left side and by its top or bottom. How far do you want the door to swing open? What kind of hinge will do what you need it to do? In chapter eleven I discuss wall and base cabinets, and talk about European or hidden hinges. These hinges have evolved into the most flexible piece of hardware available. You can hang doors that are full and half overlay, inset or flush mounted, with a 90° to 270° opening radius, with hinge plates that will mount on face frames or on the inside of the cabinet side. The hardware can be adjusted to move the doors sideways, up and down or in and out. And all of this can be done after the door has been hung on the cabinet.

There are the standard butt hinges, wraparound butt hinges, continuous butt or piano hinges, face-frame mounting

This is hinge hardware in action. Clockwise from the upper left: pivot hinge, butt hinge, hidden hinges and a set of knockdown hardware.

hinges (most kitchens use these hinges), knife hinges, pivot hinges and hidden hinges. Depending on the look you want for your cabinet or box, all of these hinges will do a great job. But they require some machining to the doors before they can be mounted and the doors hung. If a butt hinge is mounted with its barrel flush with the front of a cabinet, the door will not open to 90°. If the barrel is located proud of the front of the cabinet, the door will swing 180°. Pivot hinges can be mounted on two corners of the door and are almost invisible. The knife hinge is similar to the pivot hinge, but it is mounted in a dado which is cut into the top and bottom edges of the door. They look very neat.

You could call this a contemporary wall cabinet and be correct. I think the term contemporary is somewhat ambiguous, however, because on the day a piece of furniture is made, it's contemporary, but after that it becomes part of history. You be the judge. This cabinet has no ornamentation, no mouldings, nothing fancy. But it looks good because of the arrangement of the doors, drawer and open storage shelf. The light-colored wood, glass doors and open shelf make this an unobtrusive cabinet that could be hung in a kitchen, bathroom, den or bedroom.

Sometimes, just simple butt and bolted joinery is effective. This chair was built in sections, which made it easier to lace. Then it was bolted together and the holes were plugged with wooden mushroom plugs.

START WITH *the* BASICS

ONCE AGAIN, GREAT IDEAS require some research, study and observation of all that is around us. I even saw a tree that inspired me to make a plant stand. Just like the composer who is always thinking about composing (even if it is subconscious), we can be on the lookout for that next idea for a piece of furniture. You might even want to consider carrying a pencil and small sketch pad.

When you've got the idea and it feels good, take it back to the basics of the piece. A table is four legs and a top; a cabinet is a box; a sideboard is a box with legs; built-in cabinets are boxes that sit on the floor or are hung on the wall — you get the idea. Don't be afraid to embellish the box or top or drawer front. Of course, this is all on paper and in your imagination. You can always change your mind; you haven't bought the materials or cut anything up yet!

What we are doing here is thinking outside the box. We are considering the possibilities of what could be and what you would like. We will further refine this thinking to match your skill levels, monetary considerations, time available and the size of your shop.

Let's move on to getting that idea down on paper. Sketching is what we do when we're still not sure how things are going to look or even what the project will turn out to be. Sharpen your pencils, grab some paper and get an eraser — you're going to need it!

A lot is going on here. There are inlays on the edges of the top, the drawer fronts, the side drawer fronts and even the tambour doors. The hardware is well chosen because it is light in color. Using this many veneers can make a piece look almost sterile, but the marble top adds an organic feel to the cabinet. The drawer locks are nicely done and add contrast to the lighter veneers.

The one outstanding feature of this chest (outside of the awesome wood grain) is the arched top drawers. It is extra work but definitely worth it. This is one of those details that needs to be sketched out on paper and eventually drawn to full scale. If you want to get the full effect of what this will look like, do a mock-up of the drawer using scrap wood.

chapter **2**

creating a drawing

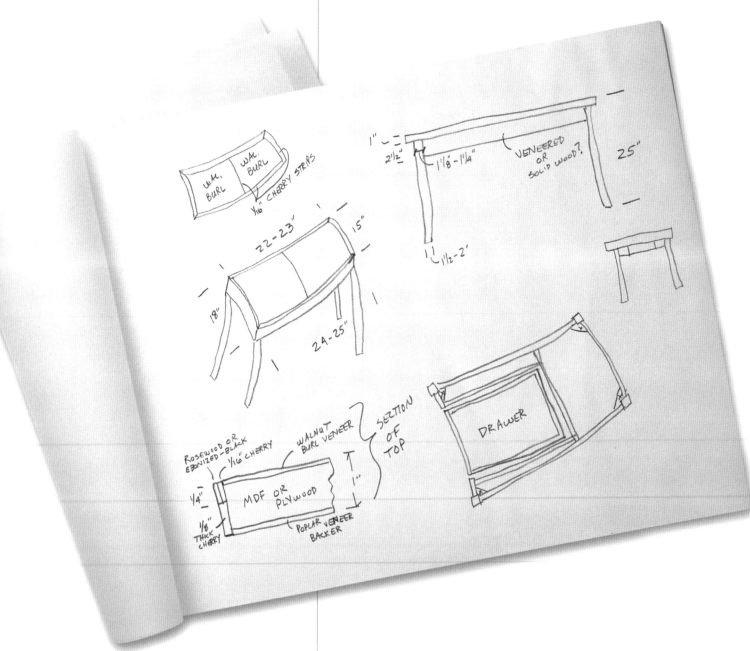

You've got an **idea**. Now what? How do you get that idea into a

workable form? Put pencil to paper, that's how!

This is a curved-leg cherry table I built for a woodworking class I was teaching. It started out as something else entirely. Only by sketching some different ideas on paper was I able to focus in on the design I was looking for. Someday, maybe I will build a table similar to the one I sketched in my original drawings. It would certainly be a different table from this one, but the design process is the same.

The sketch on page 18 shows some of the shapes I was originally thinking of making. Because this piece was to be a teaching project, I needed to keep it simple but challenging. After creating the sketches, I thought it would be nice to have a more organic piece, one that was made of only hardwood, no veneers. Veneered pieces usually have a more structured feel, with lines that are a little harder and more defined by the edges of the veneer.

When I tell folks to put their ideas on paper, they tell me they can't draw. I tell them "You don't have to be Picasso or Monet to draw!" If you can hold a pencil, you can sketch. It may not be pretty, but it will get you started on visualizing what it is you want to build.

After you've done some research and the idea has taken hold in your mind, it's time to sketch the idea on paper. As you draw, the questions will form: How large is this piece going to be? Where will it go, and will it fit there? Will it do what it is supposed to do?

Take measurements of the space this piece will occupy. Everything occupies space, so make sure it will fit where it is supposed to fit. This applies to cabinets, tables, dressers, beds, chairs, anything you build.

I recommend that you make full-scale drawings whenever the dimensions are critical, such as a cabinet that will be mounted between two walls. Full-scale drawings also give you the ability to work out special joinery problems that could arise.

When you make a mistake on paper, you can erase it and start over. Also, as you're drawing, you are building the piece in your mind, and construction details will become clear. This makes all the difference when you're in the shop concentrating on the safety details and material-handling problems that can arise. You will be clear as to how you want to build the piece, and these other distractions can more easily be dealt with.

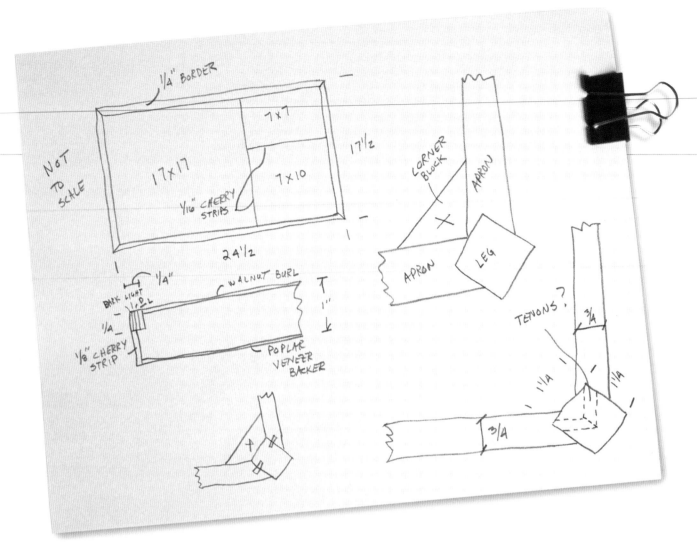

When I first started as a cabinetmaker, the first drawing I was given was a sketch with some numbers on it. I asked my boss, "What is this?" and he said it was my working drawing. I learned a lot that day. The first thing I did was build the project wrong. The second thing I did was tell my boss I just goofed. He explained to me in very clear terms that I was to use the drawing as my only source of information. He said it was all there, I just needed to understand it: He was right.

That really wasn't the whole story, but it's close. I did learn that it's important to study the drawings and become so familiar with them that you can close your eyes and still see them. My point is this: Make the mistakes in your head and get them sorted out the best you can before you

ever cut anything. I can't say this enough. The last thing you want to do is miscut that gorgeous material you've just purchased with your hard-earned money!

Let's say you're going to build a table unlike any table you've ever seen. Well, okay, let's build a small table with four legs and a top. You've decided this will be a lamp table, side table or nightstand. I designed a small table for a project in a woodworking class I was teaching at a local hardwood supplier. I will walk you through my thought processes and show you how the design came together.

A blank piece of paper can be intimidating. It just sits there waiting for you to draw something. I started by drawing a square for the top, then played with that shape for a while. One thing I did want on this table were some curved parts. I

These are detail sketches. I was brainstorming, trying some different configurations of possible ways to assemble the table at the leg and apron joint. I was also thinking about creating a veneered top with a banded border. The upper left rectangular layout is based on the golden section: The 7"-square inlay is proportional to the 7" x 10" inlay, which is proportional to the 17" square, which is proportional to the whole top. The design was becoming too stiff, so I changed direction and finally settled on the curved-leg cherry table.

This drawer is made with dovetails cut using a router and a template. Dovetails are always a good choice when using woods that are contrasting colors. The drawer glides are on hardwood strips attached to the drawer opening rails. The solid-wood top can still breathe because it is attached to the base with screws inserted in oversized holes. These holes were drilled in the cleats that are attached to the rails. When it expands and contracts with changes in humidity, the drawer will still glide.

wasn't sure which parts to curve, so I started with the top and drew several different ideas.

Then I started thinking what the top could be made of. Would it be solid wood or veneered? What would be the treatment on the edges if the top were veneered? If the edges of the top were curved, either solid wood or veneer could be used on the edges. Veneer would be easier because it would follow the curves easily. Back to sketching. I decided to keep straight edges on the top. The only other parts on this table would be the legs and the aprons. I could put a curve on the bottom of the aprons, but that wasn't what I really wanted. Of course, only after I drew it did I realize that.

That leaves the legs. This is a small table, so curving the legs in a compound

curve (two directions at the same time) seemed like the thing to do, but I've made this kind of leg before and they take some time to make. I didn't want it to be too complicated or cumbersome for the class. Then I thought, why not bend the leg to shape? That would be easier, and it was something that the class would be interested in learning. But bending can be done only in one plane, and I wanted a compound curve on the legs. More thinking and sketching.

Then it came to me: Why not fool the eye? If the leg was turned at a 45° angle to the aprons, it was possible that it would look like a compound curve. I started drawing this idea and realized that I needed to make a prototype of this leg and apron arrangement. But before I did that I would need to figure out what type

of joint would work for attaching the legs to the aprons. So I continued to sketch.

I decided that the table should have a drawer. Okay, where does the drawer fit in this design? The tabletop was originally square, but to make the drawer more functional, I decided to make the top a rectangle and put the drawer on one of the short sides. It seemed more natural to look for a drawer that would open and close the long way. If I had made the drawer to open the short length of the top, it would not have been fully accessible and would probably get pulled all the way out too often.

By adding the drawer, the table just got more complicated. The drawer needed runners, so how should I do that? You guessed it, more sketching. I needed to come up with a way to keep the leg

This table is made from scrap wood I had in my shop. The legs are strips of wood from several different boards, but they blended together in color fairly well after the table had been exposed to natural light. The drawer front was cut from the same piece as the small apron pieces on either side of it. This is a nice detail that blends the parts together visually. A drawer front in a contrasting wood would also work nicely.

structure intact and still have a drawer. After sketching a couple of possibilities I came up with a plan.

A stretcher connecting the two long aprons would give some support to the structure, and it would function as a drawer stop. There was one other idea that I liked. I wanted the legs to have a taper. How was I going to do this? I didn't need to sketch it; I just needed to figure out how to do it. I had already decided I would cut some wood into thin strips, bend them around a curved form and laminate them together. But if I cut or sanded the taper on these legs it would expose some glue lines, and I didn't want that. The solution was to cut tapered strips and glue them together as I would any laminated bend.

From a simple table with four legs and

a top, I sure had complicated things! By drawing the various ideas on paper, I was able to think things through and build the table on paper and in my mind. This made it easier to build the table, because now I had a plan. I drew a full-scale layout of the legs so I could get a feel for what they would look like. I then took this drawing and used it for a pattern to make the bending form for the legs.

During the construction, I discovered that some things went smoothly and others were still tricky, even though I had planned everything out carefully. The bending of the legs went well. No problems with that. Making the joints at the legs and aprons was a little more complicated. The ends of the aprons were cut at a 45° angle. I had to set the aprons and legs into position, upside

down on my workbench and look at things for a while. It occurred to me that the biscuit joiner was the tool for this joint. It was then a simple job to cut the slots into the legs and the ends of the aprons. I rigged up a clamping jig, and it all came together nicely.

One major design element happened during the assembly process. I made the tabletop from solid wood. I cut it with square corners and placed it on the table base, but it didn't look right. It seemed like a boring top was just stuck on this cool-looking base. After looking at the table from several different angles, it occurred to me that the top needed beveled edges. This would help complete the curve of the legs when your eye made that upward sweep. I cut bevels on the edges; that was what had been missing.

Adding a drawer made the construction more complicated. With no drawer, this table is very easy to build. I chose to put the drawer on one of the narrow ends of the table. This makes a deeper drawer that is able to be opened farther than if it was installed on the long side. The framework holds the table solidly. The screws in the cleats are inserted into oversized holes that let the top move with the seasons. This will allow the drawer and frame to stay the same even when the top moves.

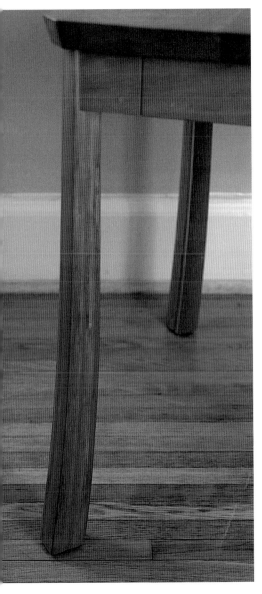

One of the reasons for making this table was to try out an idea I had. I wanted a leg with a simple bend to look like it was cut in a compound pattern. By setting the leg at a 45° angle to the aprons, the look was achieved. The leg is made of tapered strips, which give it a flare at the bottom. It is also tapered on the sides after the leg is squared up. The top of the leg is 1¼" square, and the bottom of it is 1⅞"-thick by 1⅝"-wide. These are easy things to do, and they all serve to add to the grace of the leg.

But it still wasn't complete. By turning the legs at a 45° angle, I had made the front edges of the legs a focal point. This was a strong visual line that needed completion at the top. I realized the corners of the top needed to be cut at a 45° angle to match the legs' faces. When I clipped the corners of the top and beveled them to match the other edges of the top, it all came together! I was amazed at how this small feature made such a difference.

I've made this table a couple of times since, and it is a fun project. One other thing I discovered is that the thickness of the top is critical. If it's too thin, the table looks bottom heavy. A ¼" thickness too thin makes all the difference.

Taking the time to conceive a project, design it and build it is still the ultimate in woodworking for me. I suspect it is also like that for many of you out there who work in your shops at all hours of the day and night.

creating
a materials list

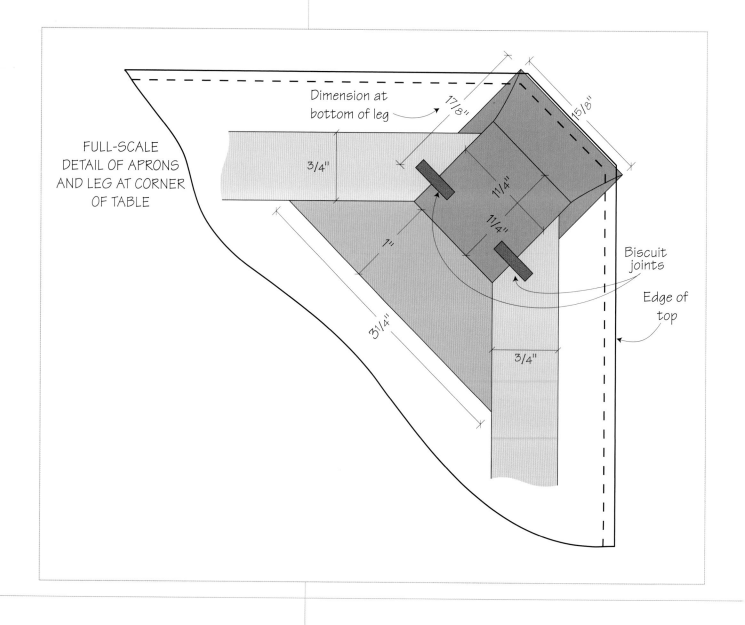

FULL-SCALE
DETAIL OF APRONS
AND LEG AT CORNER
OF TABLE

Dimension at
bottom of leg

17/8"

15/8"

3/4"

11/4"

11/4"

1"

Biscuit
joints

Edge of
top

31/4"

3/4"

You've got the **drawings**, now you need to make a list of the materials and parts

that your **furniture project** requires.

Wood is the material of choice for most furniture makers. It's interesting to be with a bunch of woodworkers when they see wood! The conversation is all about grain patterns, moisture content, workability, density and splinters.

When you're building a piece of furniture or a cabinet, creating the list of parts and materials is important. It will be your key to determining how much and what kinds of materials you will need, what hardware you'll need and how much it's all going to cost.

By taking the time to make a cutting bill, you save time in the shop. Also, you will get an even clearer idea of what all the parts will look like and how they will fit together.

As I became more experienced as a cabinetmaker, I was given more responsibility in the shop. One of the most exciting things I can remember was when my boss came to me with a set of plans and said, "Here, build these cabinets and let me know what materials I will need to order for the job." I was entrusted with the task of determining what and how much to order for the job. Granted, it wasn't my own money and the final cost of the job had already been determined, but it was important that I get it right. It was up to me to decide how the cabinets were to be constructed. I was in charge of the project!

The last shop I worked in was great. I

When you get into the shop, you don't want to be wondering what size to cut your project parts. Having an accurate cutting list is essential. When you reach this point, you should have a very clear picture of what all the parts will look like and what the project will look like when it's completed. Sketch out any special parts and have all dimensions on the sketch, so you can have fun cutting and building!

was given large projects, whether it be a residential kitchen, office or restaurant, and was responsible to see that that project was done on time, done right and done with the materials that had been ordered for the job. A lot of the materials were expensive, and it would take only one wrong cut to really make a mess of things.

I had learned the importance of carefully making a cutting list of every part that would be needed. I usually had a few people to help me with the actual construction, but in the end, it all needed to fit together and fit into the home or office for which it had been built. That was my responsibility.

When I was making the curved-leg cherry table for my class, I needed to figure out what parts and how much material would be needed. This table wasn't large, but it still required four legs, four

aprons, a top, a drawer and framework for the drawer to slide into.

The top was the first part I dimensioned. Next were the four legs, two long aprons, two short aprons (one to be cut into three pieces to yield a drawer front), four corner blocks, one stretcher, two drawer opening sides, two drawer runners, four cleats, two drawer sides, one drawer back and one drawer bottom. Wow, all this for a small table with a drawer! I'll say it again — you don't want any surprises in the middle of a project that might cost you extra because you didn't have enough materials.

The legs were a certain width and length, but when bending wood, you want to allow extra length so all the laminations can be trimmed to length after the leg has been glued together.

All hardwood is sold by the board

foot, so when figuring how much hardwood to purchase, you'll need to convert the amounts to board feet. A board foot (bf) is a unit of measure that is 1"-thick by 12"-wide by 12"-long.

For this table, I knew I wanted a top that was thicker than 1", so I needed to have a piece of wood 1½" thick to start with. That means to figure the board footage, I needed to find the area of the top, then multiply that by 1½. I decided to use 6/4 rough-sawn lumber. I could then plane down this 6/4 (1½"-thick) lumber to the thickness I wanted. If I purchased 4/4 (1"-thick) rough lumber, I would have to glue two pieces of this wood together to get the proper thickness. This is a good solution, but a glue line would show on the edge of the top.

See "Creating the Materials List for a Curved-Leg Cherry Table" on page 28 for

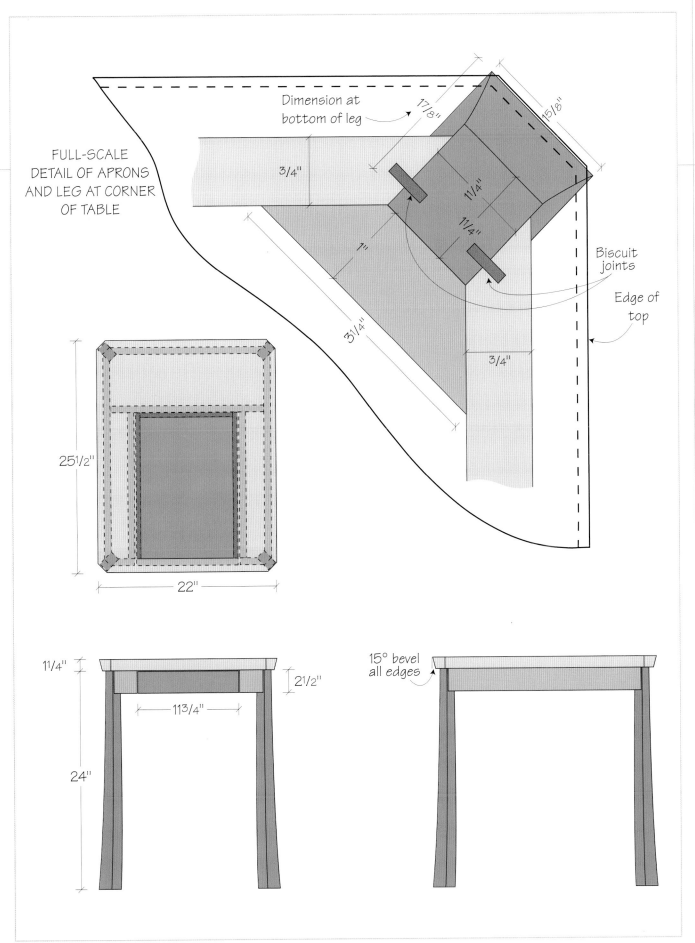

FULL-SCALE
DETAIL OF APRONS
AND LEG AT CORNER
OF TABLE

Dimension at
bottom of leg

1 7/8"

1 5/8"

3/4"

1 1/4"

1 1/4"

1"

3 1/4"

3/4"

Biscuit
joints

Edge of
top

25 1/2"

22"

1 1/4"

2 1/2"

11 3/4"

24"

15° bevel
all edges

creating the materials list for a curved-leg cherry table

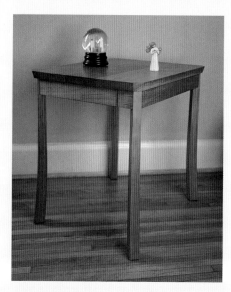

The materials list for your project will be your guide for the materials needed, the quantities of each and the cost.

I start at the top of a project and work my way down. For example, if it's a cabinet I will size the top, then the sides, bottom, rails, base, back, doors and drawers.

Let's create the materials list for the curved-leg cherry table. It has one top $1\frac{1}{4}$"-thick by 22"-wide by $25\frac{1}{2}$"-long. Next are four legs, which are going to be bent. Each leg will be made of ten $1\frac{3}{8}$"-wide by 26"-long strips tapering from $\frac{3}{16}$" to $\frac{1}{8}$", which will make a leg $1\frac{3}{8}$"-wide by approximately $25\frac{1}{2}$"-long, tapering from $1\frac{7}{8}$" at the bottom to $1\frac{1}{4}$" at the top.

Two $\frac{3}{4}$"-thick by $2\frac{1}{2}$"-wide by $22\frac{1}{2}$"-long aprons, two $\frac{3}{4}$"-thick by $2\frac{1}{2}$"-wide by $17\frac{1}{4}$"-long aprons, four corner blocks 1"-thick by $2\frac{1}{2}$"-wide by $3\frac{1}{4}$"-long, and four $\frac{3}{4}$"-square by 10"-long cleats complete the parts necessary to make the table.

The drawer is made of two sides $\frac{1}{2}$"-thick by $2\frac{3}{8}$"-wide by $16\frac{5}{16}$"-long, one back $\frac{1}{2}$"-thick by $2\frac{3}{8}$"-wide by $11\frac{1}{2}$"-long, one drawer front $\frac{3}{4}$"-thick by $2\frac{3}{8}$"-wide by $11\frac{7}{8}$"-long, and one bottom $\frac{1}{2}$"-thick by $11\frac{3}{8}$"-wide by $16\frac{1}{2}$"-long. There are two drawer opening rails $\frac{3}{4}$"-thick by $2\frac{1}{2}$"-wide by 16"-long, and one cross support rail $\frac{3}{4}$"-thick by $2\frac{1}{2}$"-wide by $17\frac{1}{2}$"-long.

The top and legs will be made from 6/4 cherry. The top measures 22" x $25\frac{1}{2}$". Multiply these two dimensions, then divide the number by 144 (the number of square inches in a square foot). This equals 3.9 square feet. Each leg will need ten strips $\frac{3}{16}$"-thick by 26"-long, but the strips will be cut on the table saw, and each time a strip is cut, $\frac{1}{8}$" of material will be wasted by the blade. This means an extra $\frac{1}{8}$" of material (or $\frac{3}{16}$" + $\frac{1}{8}$" = $\frac{5}{16}$" total) will be needed for each strip. So multiply $\frac{5}{16}$" or 0.3125 by 26" and divide by 144; multiply this by 10 (for the ten strips). Each leg will thus require 0.6 square feet of material, so four legs will require 2.4 square feet of material. Add 3.9 and 2.4, which

equals 6.3 square feet of material needed for the top and legs. To be sure you'll have enough material, add about 10 to 20 percent, which will be 7 to $7\frac{1}{2}$ square feet of material. Since we're using 6/4 material, we need to multiply this by $1\frac{1}{2}$, which means you will need $10\frac{1}{2}$ to $11\frac{1}{4}$ board feet of 6/4 cherry.

The aprons and corner blocks are also made of cherry, but they can be made from 4/4 material. The amount of material needed is figured the same way as for the top and legs, but the final square footage of material needed for these parts will also equal the board footage needed. Remember that a board foot is 1"-thick by 12"-wide by 12"-long.

The drawer material, soft maple, will also come from 4/4 stock, because rough lumber is sold in thicknesses no smaller than 4/4. The drawer front is cut from one of the short aprons so the grain pattern will match. The plywood for the drawer bottom is figured in square footage no matter what the thickness of the material is. You can purchase $\frac{1}{4}$, $\frac{1}{2}$ and whole 4x8 sheets of plywood at any home-improvement center.

The total amount of materials needed for this project are:

$11\frac{1}{4}$ board feet of 6/4 cherry

2 board feet of 4/4 cherry

2 board feet of 4/4 soft maple

1.3 square feet of $\frac{1}{4}$"-thick plywood

This is what your cutting list will look like when you're done with all of your calculations:

CUTTING LIST

QTY.	PART	MATERIAL	T	W	L
1	Top	6/4 cherry	$1^{1}/_{4}$	22	$25^{1}/_{2}$
4	Legs	6/4 cherry	$1^{1}/_{4}$ to $1^{7}/_{8}$	$1^{1}/_{4}$ to $1^{3}/_{8}$	24
2	Side Aprons	4/4 cherry	$^{3}/_{4}$	$2^{1}/_{2}$	$22^{1}/_{2}$
2	End Aprons	4/4 cherry	$^{3}/_{4}$	$2^{1}/_{2}$	$17^{1}/_{4}$
4	Corner Blocks	4/4 soft maple	1	$2^{1}/_{2}$	$3^{1}/_{4}$
4	Cleats	4/4 soft maple	$^{3}/_{4}$	$^{3}/_{4}$	10
2	Drawer Sides	4/4 soft maple	$^{1}/_{2}$	$2^{3}/_{8}$	$16^{5}/_{16}$
1	Drawer Back	4/4 soft maple	$^{1}/_{2}$	$2^{3}/_{8}$	$11^{1}/_{2}$
1	Drawer Bottom	plywood	$^{1}/_{4}$	$11^{3}/_{8}$	$16^{1}/_{2}$
1	Drawer Front	4/4 cherry	$^{3}/_{4}$	$2^{3}/_{8}$	$11^{7}/_{8}$
2	Drawer Glides	4/4 soft maple	$^{1}/_{4}$	$^{1}/_{2}$	16
2	Drawer Opening Rails	4/4 soft maple	$^{3}/_{4}$	$2^{1}/_{2}$	16
1	Cross Support Rail	4/4 soft maple	$^{3}/_{4}$	$2^{1}/_{2}$	$17^{1}/_{2}$

Make notes as to what special cuts are needed for each part. For example, all the aprons will be cut 45° at each end. The length of the legs in the cutting list is the *finished* length. All the cleats are cut at 45° on both ends. The corners of the top will be clipped at 45°, and then all the edges of the top will be beveled 15°. Remember to cut the dado in both of the drawer sides *after* you cut the dovetails, but *before* you assemble the drawer.

When making this table, you will need to make a jig for bending the legs and special clamping blocks for assembly of the legs and aprons.

This is a lot of information to remember; that's why you write it all down. It may seem like busywork now, but when you're in the middle of cutting, bending, gluing and routing, you'll be glad you have a guide. This is a small project. Just think how many pieces there are to a large built-in bookcase or a couple of kitchen cabinets!

Don't be intimidated, just be thorough!

wood types guide

COLOR	WOOD	COST	NOTES
White	Aspen	$	Soft and easily worked. Can have streaks of brown.
	Silver Maple	$$	Hard; stable. Machines and takes finish very well.
	Spruce (Adirondack spruce, blue spruce, skunk spruce)	$	Soft and easily worked. Grain has a strong character.
	Eastern white pine	$	Pines have high pitch content that can ruin blades — use blade lubricant. Soft and easy to work but can split easily.
	Sugar pine	$$	Close, consistent grain. Soft; easy to work. Carves very well.
	Western white pine	$	See above for eastern white pine.
	Holly	$$$	Discolors if the wood is not cut properly. Very nice white color.
	Basswood (American lime)	$	Turns pale brown on exposure. Soft; closed grained. Carves well.
	Hard maple (rock maple, sugar maple)	$$	Hard; stable. Machines and takes finish very well.
	European ash (English/French/etc. ash)	$$	Turns light brown on exposure. Machines well.
Black	Black walnut	$$	Medium hard and can be carved. Turns reddish brown over time.
	Wenge	$$$	Hard; brittle. Nice brown color but dust is very irritating.
	South American walnut	$$$	Light brown; medium hardness. Machines well.
	Ebony (gaboon)	$$$	Hard; endangered. Browns to black. Good accent wood.
Red	Bloodwood (Brazil redwood, cardinal wood, pau rainha)	$$$	Nice red color; hard; brittle. Holds color.
	Aromatic cedar (eastern red cedar, chest cedar, Tennessee cedar)	$	Reddish brown knots with whitish wood. Splits easily; lots of resin in the knots. If finished it loses its aroma.
	Cherry	$$	Medium hard; can be carved. Turns deep brownish red.
	Jarrah	$$	Moderately difficult to work. Takes finish well.
	Brazilwood (pernambuco wood, bahia wood, para wood)	$$$	Hard; brittle; deep reddish brown colors.
	African padauk (camwood, barwood)	$$	Medium hard; brittle. Turns burgundy color. Dust is irritating.
	Redheart	$$$	Rich red color; medium hard; brittle. Machines well. Holds color.
Yellow	Pau amarillo	$$	Brightest — canary yellow.
	Orange osage	$$	Turns orange-brown on exposure.
	Yellow cedar (Alaska cedar, nootka cypress, yellow cypress)	$$	Soft; easy to work. Carves easily. Usually has nice straight grain.
	Yellow pine	$	Hard, heavy, tough and very strong grain pattern.
	Ponderosa pine (western yellow pine, Californian white pine)	$	Hard, heavy, tough and very strong grain pattern.
	Caragana	$	Actually a shrub — have to look for it.
	Hickory	$$	Hard; light brown to brown. Bends well. Brittle; heavy.
	Yellowheart	$$	Hard. Holds color fairly well.
	Satinwood (East Indian satinwood)	$$$	Hard; somewhat brittle; moderately difficult to work.
	Obeche (ayous, wawa, arere)	$	Hard; somewhat brittle; moderately difficult to work.
Green	Staghorn sumac (velvet sumac)	$	Difficult to find.
	American yellow poplar (tulip tree, canary wood, canoe wood)	$	Medium hard; light brown, green and purple. Machines well.
	Vera wood (Maracaibo, lignum vitae, guyacan)	$$$	Hard; oily; close grain. Machines well.
Blue/Gray	Spruce (Adirondack spruce, blue spruce, skunk spruce)	$	Some spruce boards have gray or blue cast.
	Blue mahoe (mahoe, mountain mahoe, seaside mahoe)	$$$	Heartwood varies from purple, metallic blue, olive brown. Must search for blue.
Purple	Purpleheart (violet wood, pauroxo, coracy)	$$	Hard; brittle. Dust is irritating. Holds color well.
Orange	Orange osage	$$	Cuts yellow, then turns orange on exposure; medium hard.
	Zebrawood	$$$	Dark streaks throughout. Soft; splits easily; good accent wood.
	Red gum (sweet gum, alligator wood, hazel pine)	$$	Streaks of red and black; beautiful grain; good accent wood.

Legend: $ Inexpensive

$$ Moderately priced

$$$ Expensive

plywood

Plywood is a versatile material and is available at all home-improvement centers and hardwood dealers. It's made in thicknesses ranging from ⅛" to 1", with the most common being ¼", ½" and ¾". All are available in 4×8 sheets. Most stores will custom-cut these sheets into smaller sizes for you if needed.

Plywood is graded by letters, with A being the best and D a reject veneer on the back of some plywood, which is fine if that side of the panel won't be seen. (It does save you some money.) An AA-BB sheet of plywood has top-quality plane-sliced (the veneer is sliced off the log lengthwise, like cutting bread into slices the long way on the loaf) veneers on one face and next-grade (BB) bookmatched veneers on the opposite face. An A-B or A-C plywood has top-quality rotary-cut (sliced off the log as the log is turned, like you would pull paper towels off the roll) veneers on the face and next-quality (B) or lesser-quality (C) rotary-cut veneer on the opposite face. There is also B-C, C-D, and CDX (exterior-grade glues are used in the plywood).

Any species of wood veneer is available on plywood. Maple, birch, red oak, ash, poplar, walnut, cherry and pine are the most common.

Every other piece is flipped like the pages of a book.

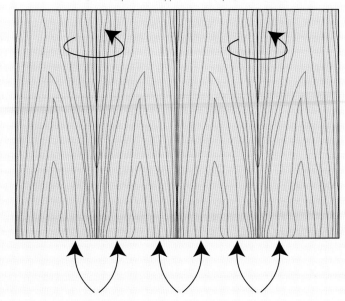

A mirror image of each piece is created by the piece next to it.

further information about how I decided the size and shape of the parts needed.

When designing furniture or cabinetry, you'll have to decide what materials you will use to build your projects.

On page 30 is a chart that tells some of the basic characteristics of the more common woods.

When working with any wood, remember to wear respiratory protection. The common nuisance masks work to a degree. They will filter most of the larger dust particles, but the smaller particles will still get into your lungs. I recommend purchasing a dust mask that has screw-in filters because these will filter microscopic particles. If you have allergies, wear a mask at all times.

Some of the imported woods contain oils and resins that can cause skin, eye and respiratory allergic reactions. Some of these reactions can be severe, with symptoms similar to poison ivy. If you have any question about the wood, wear gloves, goggles and a dust mask, or don't use the wood.

Many exotic woods can be purchased as veneers, which can be used without having to cut them with power saws and creating dust. Also, the process of making veneers changes the wood slightly and makes it much safer to work with. When logs are sliced into veneer, they are first soaked or saturated with water to make the wood more pliable and easier to slice. This soaking process causes the wood to lose oils and resins. In fact, Antonio Stradivari, the world-famous violin maker, used to soak his sound board woods in water to remove the resins because it would make the wood vibrate with a warmer and clearer sound.

Another characteristic of any wood is that it will change shape and size with humidity. There is absolutely no way to stop this movement. In fact, rocks and boulders can be split by driving wooden wedges into cracks; then the wood is soaked with water and swells. As the crack becomes larger, thicker wedges are used until the rock splits.

When designing furniture that will require large panels of wood, try to use plywood panels. Plywood does not change with humidity. It is stable and strong, so it won't warp or split.

Plywood is available in many varieties and thicknesses. Bookmatched veneers are available on all thicknesses of plywood. Using bookmatched veneers gives a piece of furniture that extra design feature that will set it apart from rotary-cut veneer.

Rotary-cut veneer has a grain pattern that never repeats. The cathedral shapes created by this slicing process can look quite dramatic.

If you'd rather use solid-wood panels, use the time-tested frame-and-panel construction technique for furniture and cabinet sides and doors. The frame will hold the panel in place, allow it to expand and contract with seasonal changes and keep it from warping.

Never glue a batten cross-grain to a solid-wood panel. This will cause the panel to warp and split. If a batten is attached, use screws driven through oversized holes in the batten. This will allow the panel to expand and contract because the screws will move in the oversized holes when the panel moves, and the batten will hold the panel flat because there is little tension on the batten.

sizing from
a photograph

You've just found the perfect piece of **furniture** that has everything you've been looking

for, only it's a **photograph** in a book. If only you knew the measurements of the piece.

Here's how you can determine those **measurements**.

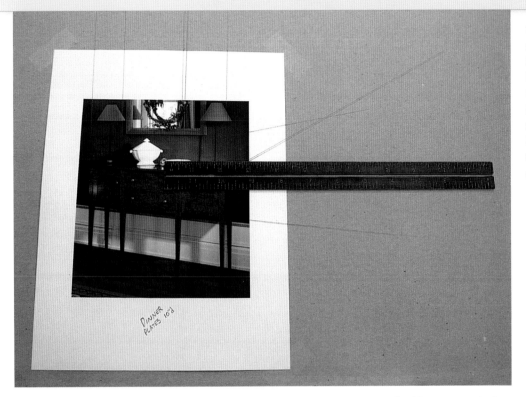

If there is a common item in the photo, measure something similar to it in real life. Then measure the object in the photo. This will give you the ratio or scale that you need to size the piece of furniture. Whenever possible, measure off of the photo itself. If this isn't possible or the photo is too small, try enlarging the photo or use the technique on the next page.

A client came to me once with a photo from a magazine and said this was the cabinet she had been looking for but couldn't find anywhere. She wanted to know if I could build the cabinet for her. I said sure, silently saying to myself, "I sure hope I can figure out what size this is supposed to be!"

I was able to build the cabinet for her, and it all went just fine. I found a starting point for a measurement because there was a chair in the photo. Knowing what the average chair seat height is, I was able to use that as a starting point for my calculations. I used an architect's scale ruler to measure, directly on the photo, the distance from the floor to the top of the chair seat. I found a scale that worked and used it to measure different parts of

the cabinet. By using my past building experience, I was able to determine a logical sizing of all the parts for the cabinet.

Now, I know that sounds oversimplified, but that's how it works. If you don't have a scale ruler, a standard or metric ruler will work just fine. What you need to do is create your own scale.

If you find a photo in a furniture book, the dimensions are usually noted in the caption. In the case of a magazine, this may not be the case. But if you encounter a photo with no dimensions, there is usually something else in the photo that will give you an idea of the size of the piece. For instance, a bookcase will probably have books in it. Using logic, you can come very close to guessing the size of the book. Compare it to books you have and measure them. If the furniture is in a room, is it next to a

window or door? Be a detective and see what you can find in the photo that will give you something to compare to the piece of furniture.

Let's say you've chosen to make the piece of furniture in the photo on page 32. Where do you start?

There are some dinner plates in the photo which average 9" to 10" in diameter. Using $\frac{1}{16}$", $\frac{1}{8}$", $\frac{1}{4}$", $\frac{1}{2}$" or metric divisions, measure the plate in the photo. This measurement is equal to the full-scale plate diameter of 10". You now have a scale or formula that will help you determine the dimensions of the other parts of the cabinet.

The first rule is to measure directly from the photo if you can. If the photo is too small, you can extend the primary lines of the cabinet.

First, place the photo on a large piece

DESIGN YOUR OWN FURNITURE

determining measurements

Multiply the measurements for each part in the photo by the fraction $^{10}/_{15}$ or .67 (in this example). 10" is the diameter of the plates and 15 is the number of increments on the ruler. This will give you the full-scale inch or millimeter measurements for each part of the cabinet. Round numbers up to common measurements, as shown below.

LEG WIDTH AT TOP - 3 x .67 = 2"

LEG WIDTH AT BOTTOM - 1.75 x .67 = 1.25"

LEG HEIGHT - 57 x .67 = 38"

WIDTH OF STEPBACK - 24 x .67 = 16"

WIDTH OF STEPOUT - 35 x .67 = 23.5"

HEIGHT OF CABINET BODY - 22 x .67 = 14.75"

BOTTOM RAIL - 1.5 x .67 = 1"

TOP RAIL - 1.25 x .67 = .75"

LENGTH OF TOP - 79 x .67 = 53"

WIDTH OF TOP IN CENTER - 16" to 18" based on just looking at the plates and making a best guess.

WIDTH OF TOP AT END - 14" to 16" based on just looking at the plates and making a best guess.

THICKNESS OF TOP - 1.25 x .67 = 75"

OVERHANG OF TOP ON CABINET - 1 x .67 = .5" to .75"

WIDTH OF DOOR - 19 x .67 = 12.75"

HEIGHT OF DOOR - 19 x .67 = 12.75"

WIDTH OF DOOR STILES AND RAILS - 3.25 x .67 = 2" to 2.25"

Extend the lines of the cabinet onto the paper. Tilt the ruler as needed to find an easy number of increments on the ruler to use as your scale. Then, draw a line against the ruler. Where this line intersects the cabinet's extended lines is where you can measure all the horizontal parts of the cabinet. Do the same thing for the vertical parts.

of paper. It could be an unfolded paper sack, a piece of cardboard or even a piece of newspaper. Use a red pen or pencil to draw lines on the newspaper so you can see them. Extend the lines of the cabinet in the photo by drawing them onto the paper or cardboard, as shown in the photos on pages 33 and 34.

Move onto the paper where you've drawn the lines and measure the plate width, tilting the ruler as needed until an even or convenient number appears. Draw a line against the ruler. By measuring along this line where it intersects the cabinet's extended lines, you can measure any horizontal part. Do this same thing for the vertical parts. The reason this works has to do with the perspective lines

being extended and keeping the same proportions as they approach the vanishing point where all the lines come together and create a black hole. (You want to avoid the black hole if you can!)

Now that you've got all these numbers, what do you do with them?

Start with the original scale measurement you had for the dinner plate in the photo. This equals 10" in full scale. Make a fraction out of these two numbers. $^{10}/x$, where x=the number you read from the ruler, which equals the plate diameter in the photo. Convert this fraction to a decimal number (10 divided by x). Multiply each measurement you get from the photo by this number. The result is equal to the number of inches each piece will

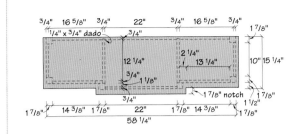

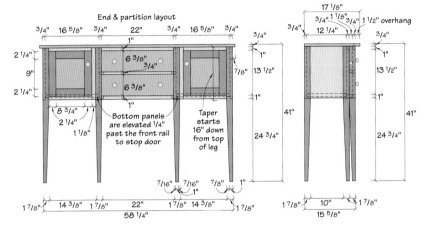

Drawing to full scale is the best way to see how the piece of furniture or cabinet is going to look. It also gives you a sense of the proportion of the project. It could very well be too big, too small or just right!

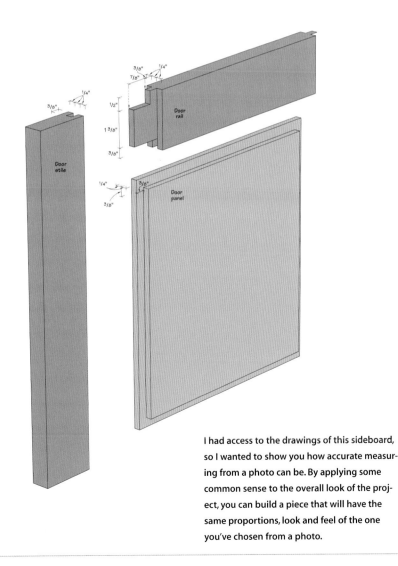

I had access to the drawings of this sideboard, so I wanted to show you how accurate measuring from a photo can be. By applying some common sense to the overall look of the project, you can build a piece that will have the same proportions, look and feel of the one you've chosen from a photo.

be in full scale.

With these full-scale measurements, you can create drawings that will help you in your quest to build this cabinet. If you find that the cabinet is not the correct size in full scale, feel free to scale it up or down in size to suit your needs.

When you're happy with the size of the cabinet, you can begin to work out construction details and draw the mouldings, joinery and other parts full scale. This is the same procedure as shown in chapter two, "Creating a Drawing."

One other design technique I will mention here is building full-scale mock-ups of certain parts or a whole project. Rather than waste your primary materials when deciding how to make a particular moulding or joint, use scrap wood or cardboard. By mocking up parts this way, you can see how the full-scale proportions will look. Many times I've changed the shape or size of a part when I saw it full size because it just didn't look like I thought it would (or should).

I've used a lot of corrugated cardboard in my career. It is great for drawing on and cutting out mocked-up parts. I also like to use inexpensive ¼" plywood or tempered hardboard. When I'm fairly certain that what I've drawn on this hardboard is what I want, I will cut it out and use the hardboard or plywood for a cutting or routing template. By spending time drawing and erasing on this ¼" material, I've worked out lots of "bugs" in a short amount of time. I'm then able to move on to construction of the project in fairly short order by having the template right there in front of me.

chapter 5

small shop
considerations

Just because you have a **small** shop doesn't mean you can't **build** what you want.

Building larger pieces will take some **special planning,** but you can do it.

SHOPS

This isn't a book about shops, but there are considerations that you, as the designer and builder of your own furniture, can think about while you're designing and getting ready to build.

Plan your cutting schedule according to how you have your shop arranged. For ex-

ample, my shop is in my garage, which is long and narrow (8'-wide by 18'-long). I also have some room in my basement that I use for assembly and hand-tool work.

Many people have told me that they would like to make a dining table or an entertainment center, but they just don't have the room or the tools. I tell them that by planning and putting things down on paper, they will be amazed at what

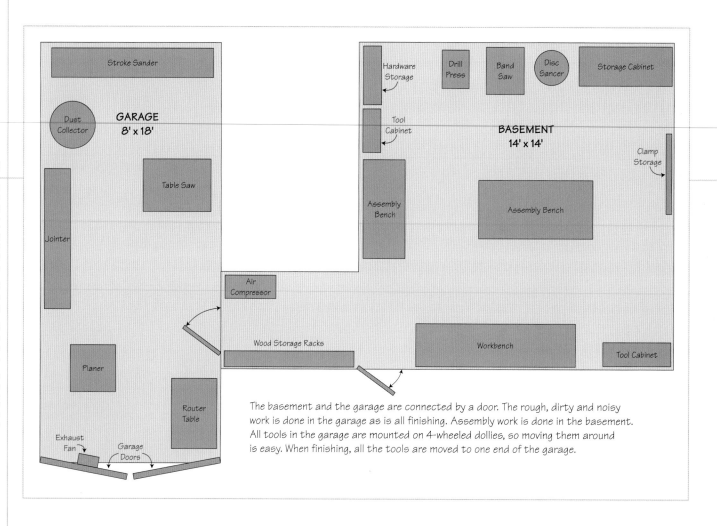

Stroke Sander

Dust Collector

GARAGE
8' x 18'

Table Saw

Jointer

Air Compressor

Planer

Wood Storage Racks

Router Table

Exhaust Fan

Garage Doors

Hardware Storage

Drill Press

Band Saw

Disc Sander

Storage Cabinet

Tool Cabinet

BASEMENT
14' x 14'

Clamp Storage

Assembly Bench

Assembly Bench

Workbench

Tool Cabinet

The basement and the garage are connected by a door. The rough, dirty and noisy work is done in the garage as is all finishing. Assembly work is done in the basement. All tools in the garage are mounted on 4-wheeled dollies, so moving them around is easy. When finishing, all the tools are moved to one end of the garage.

they can do in a small shop with a minimum amount of tools. It may take a little longer to build a project in some cases, but the results are just as good no matter what tools are used.

Back when I first started woodworking, I had no shop and only five tools: a circular saw, a power hand drill, a hammer, a screwdriver and a combination square. I built my first workbench with these tools. I built it outside on a patio and worked when I wouldn't disturb my neighbors.

I was able to build that bench because I carefully planned the whole project start to finish. I drew plans and figured how much and what kind of wood I would need. I accounted for every cutoff of wood and used them to make other parts of the bench. It was complete with drawers that had dadoes for the bottoms to slide into. I was proud of my accomplishment, and it was a good bench that

served me well. When I moved from the house, I left the bench for the next tenant, so I hope it's had a good life.

I now have a complete set of stationary power tools, plus lots of hand tools. I don't have a large shop, however. It occupies about two-thirds of my basement.

I built an 8' × 14' conference table, complete with massive legs, and I was able to get it out of the house! I've also built large armoires, dressers and bookcases. My point is this, large pieces of furniture can be built in a small shop if all things are carefully planned.

I realize that some of you fellow woodworkers out there don't have a lot of space. Maybe you have just a closet in the basement or you work in the laundry room on nonlaundry days. If you want to build a full set of kitchen cabinets, you definitely need to plan carefully, even if you have to build one cabinet at a time.

Making knockdown furniture is the

best way to make large things. You can build one part at a time, move all the parts where you need them and then put it all together like a puzzle.

I remember repairing a very large (over 8' tall) antique armoire for a client. It could be taken apart to be moved. It had two side pieces, a top with moulding, a base, a middle fixed shelf, a back, two large raised-panel doors and several adjustable shelves. The doors had loose-pin hinges, which made removing the doors easy. The sides had wooden blocking that lined up with notches in the top and bottom parts. Screws were used to hold it all together. The back panel fit into rabbets in the back edges of the sides and was screwed into place. This ornate piece of furniture was in no way shabby-looking or rickety. I was impressed with the engineering of the piece and thought that more furniture should be made like this!

The European or 32mm cabinetmak-

You will be amazed at what you can do in a small shop with a minimum amount of tools.

ing system is clever, practical and it saves your lower back. (For more on this system, see chapter eleven, "Wall and Base Cabinets.") Most of the cabinetry made using this system is for kitchens, but I believe that it has application in furniture making as well. Those of us in our small shops could use this system to good advantage!

I have a table saw, jointer, planer and router table in the garage. My garage is under the house and has a concrete ceiling, sides and floor. Using these machines in the garage helps me control the dust and noise when I machine parts.

When I start a project, I rip all of the lumber and sheet materials first. The table saw is mounted on a 4-wheeled dolly, so I can move it around easily. I turn the saw so I can feed the material the length of the garage. After all ripping is done, I turn the table saw 90° and crosscut the parts to length. This includes any hardwood, which I cut to rough length.

The jointer and planer are also mounted on dollies. The jointer is against one long wall, so I can access it easily. After jointing all the hardwood parts, I move the table saw out of the way, pull the thickness planer into position and plane all hardwood parts to the correct width and thickness. I also have a dust collector for these tools, which is an absolute must for anyone who owns a jointer or planer. I do all routing and shaping in the garage also.

After I have machined all the parts, I do the "cleaner" work in the basement. I then return to the garage to apply the finishes. I roll all the tools to one end of the garage and set up the finishing station. An exhaust fan is mounted in the door so

In a small shop, putting your heavy stationary power tools on rollers is very helpful. Moving these tools is essential if space is limited. On rollers or casters, one person can very easily move a heavy tool.

all fumes can be drawn outside.

I think 90 percent of us who have shops in our homes can relate to this scenario I've just shared. If the desire is strong enough, you can always find a way to make what you want in the space that you have available.

It takes patience to build a project one part at a time. But if you have your cutting bill in front of you, you know exactly what the dimensions of each part are and what special machining (drilling, shaping, cutting, mitering) needs to be done. By making each part separately and doing as much as you can to make that part complete, you can manage a large project. The final assembly may need to be done in another location, but moving a bunch of small parts is easier than moving one big project.

It you don't have a jointer or planer, most woodworking stores will sell you dimensioned lumber. Some local cabinet shops will plane or thickness-sand lumber

for you. Offer to pay them and they will probably tell you to stop by during lunchtime when the workers aren't using the machines.

When you are planning your project, try to use standard-size materials so you won't need to have special machining done. Also, use all the standard mouldings you can. By combining different mouldings, you can create some very nice looking "custom" mouldings.

Standard thicknesses of dimensioned hardwoods are $\frac{1}{2}$", $\frac{3}{4}$", $1\frac{1}{4}$" and $1\frac{1}{2}$". Widths are usually $1\frac{1}{2}$", $2\frac{1}{2}$", $3\frac{1}{2}$", $4\frac{1}{2}$", $5\frac{1}{2}$" and so on. Be sure to take a tape measure with you whenever you go shopping for materials, so you won't be surprised when you get home and find the wood isn't the size you or the clerk thought it was.

And remember to enjoy the journey, because that's why we started woodworking in the first place!

putting it all together

When Amy, a co-worker, came to me and said she would like to make a media cabinet, I asked her if she knew what she wanted, or if she wanted to start from the very beginning. She said she "sort of" knew, but wanted to know if I had any "ideas."

I told her to start by getting the measurements of all the electronic equipment she wanted to put into the cabinet. When she came back the next day with all the dimensions, I knew she was serious, so I gave her some books and magazines that had lots of ideas for media centers.

After looking through all the materials, she came back with some sketches. I was impressed that she had put some of her ideas on paper. We looked through them and decided to take some elements of one idea and put it with another. Eventually we had created a cabinet concept. It fit her needs and was in a style that she liked.

Since she lives in a small apartment, I suggested that she make the cabinet from a light-colored wood so it wouldn't appear too large. She agreed, and then she asked me if I would help her build the cabinet.

I agreed, so the process of creating a materials list, cutting list and hardware list commenced. When we finished, we knew what we needed and in what quantities. After trips to the wood store and to the hardware store, we were ready to start making some sawdust.

We spent about two and a half months of lunch hours building the media cabi-

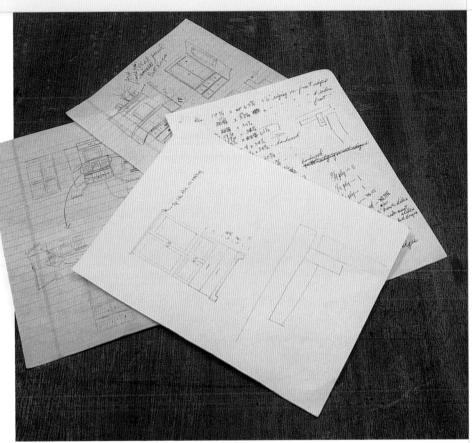

net. It was a test of patience for us because it's tough to get much done in such short blocks of time. What made it easier was the fact that we had it all on paper and could start right where we left off each time. There were times when neither of us was available for several days in a row, so it was a good test of how organized we were. We old guys tend to forget what we were doing five minutes ago, so Amy would help me remember what we had been doing the last time we worked!

What follows is the project from start to finish. It is my hope that this will help you see how the whole process of designing, planning, drawing, creating a materials list, building and finishing can proceed smoothly.

step one After the cabinet parts are cut out, glue ¼" x ¹³/₁₆" hardwood strips to the front edges of all the shelves and sides. These strips cover the plywood and provide protection for the edges of the veneer.

step two When the glue has dried, trim the strips flush to the surface of the plywood with a block plane, or a router set up with a flush trimming bit. Be careful not to nick the veneer. Sand the joint smooth.

step three Lay out where the fixed shelves will be attached to the sides and cut double slots for #20 biscuits. These double slots provide tremendous holding power for the fixed shelves. Then cut the matching slots in the ends of the shelves.

step four Glue the front base onto the cabinet first, then the side pieces. Take your time to cut and fit the miter joints where the front meets the sides.

step five   We made a template for the cutout on the front base piece and used it to guide a router with a straight cutting bit. This step could be done before the base is glued into place, but this seemed easier because the base was already in place and it was easy to make this router setup.

step six   After cutting the grooves in the stiles and rails for the doors (make sure the ¼" door panels fit into the grooves!), cut the tenons. We used a dado-cutting setup in the table saw, but using a single blade will work also. Just nibble the material away a little at a time. In either case, set the saw's fence so you will be cutting the full length of the tenon when the end of the rail is against the fence.

step seven   When assembling the doors, do it on a flat surface. This will ensure your door will be flat when you glue it together. Always check the door for square by measuring the diagonals. When they are equal, the door is square. If the door isn't square, loosen the clamps and skew them slightly to pull the door square.

step eight   We decided to use pivot hinges on the doors. These allow the doors to lay almost flat against the sides of the cabinet when they are open. When the doors are closed, the hinges are hardly noticeable, which fits in with the straight-lined, flat-panel look of the cabinet.

chapter **7**

beds, dressers
sideboards and hutches

This Tansu bedside table is a gem of a piece. Its design is subtle in places and bold in others. Construction is basic mortise and tenon. The open area under the top, the front and back rails on the top, and the multi-railed sliding doors give this table its distinctive look. Because of the plain-sawn maple, the table has a light look and the lines are crisp.

This is the **furniture** that we live with day-in and day-out, so it's important that

we have **great designs** that fit our personal **needs and styles**.

The Sheraton field bed is a great example of a bed that is completely knockdown. It comes apart into four posts, two side rails, two foot/head rails and a headboard. The turned and fluted posts are graceful and override any other design detail on this bed. It is sometimes made with a canopy, which gives the bed an extra feeling of comfort and privacy.

BEDS

Beds are like chairs; they occupy and put definition on a certain space. This space is mostly air, but we know that the area around, below and above a bed or chair is reserved for that piece of furniture only.

The average person will spend one-third of his or her life sleeping. In times past, people were generally shorter than they are now. The beds were shorter, of course, but they sometimes weren't even long enough for a person to lie down full length. While researching this book I learned that people used more pillows and slept in a sitting position, hence the beds were shorter! Our sleeping positions have changed, and beds are now long enough for very tall people to lie down comfortably.

Out of necessity, beds are knockdown pieces of furniture, consisting of a headboard, footboard and side rails that connect the two. The side rails have cleats that support a submattress or box springs. Slats are usually laid across these cleats to give added support.

In families with several members, beds can be built one on top of another. These bunk beds are a great way to save space.

Many of us who went to college had limited room to study, so we created our own loft beds. The bed was on tall legs, and the space under was used to house a desk or table and chair.

A bed needs to support the full weight of one or more people, so good joinery is essential. Frame and panel construction techniques can be used to make headboards and footboards. The legs are connected to rails or panels using mortise-and-tenon, biscuit, or dowel joinery. The side rails are attached to the bed using knockdown hardware or bolts, as shown in the photos below.

This is a set of bed rail hardware. Each part is set into a mortise. When the hooks are slipped into the slots, the rail is pulled tightly against the bed post.

Using two dowels and a bolt to secure a bed rail to the headboard and footboard creates a strong joint. This joint can be taken apart easily.

Murphy beds are a good solution if you don't need to have a bed all the time. This version is well done: a cabinet complete with bookshelves and base cabinet storage.

When guests need a place to sleep, it is a simple matter to set up the bed. The bookcase and base cabinet storage is still intact, and a good night's sleep awaits your guests.

Here's another solution when a bed isn't needed all the time. This futon is based on a design taken from a book on Mormon furniture. In the early 1800s, lounges like this were popular in eastern Canada and the United States. Once pioneers started migrating west in the United States, they took their furniture-building ideas with them. This futon is called a *double lounge* because the front of the base can be pulled straight out to double the depth of the lounge. An extra cushion is then added and two people can rest comfortably.

The modern version of this double lounge works well with a futon mattress. It only takes about 10 seconds to pull the base front out and slide the mattress into place. Interlocking slats provide the support for the mattress. A stop block halts the movement when maximum extension has been reached.

Some people prefer a cabinlike atmosphere. This bed is made from rough-sawn pine in a simple, straight-line design. The assembly bolt heads have been left exposed. The spindles aren't needed for structure; they simply add some vertical lines for the headboard and footboard. Even if this bed was placed in a room without real-pine wall paneling, it would give the space that "rustic" feeling.

This huntboard contrasts with the piece below, making a totally different statement. Why? What is different about this cabinet from the one below? It has legs, drawers, doors and a top, doesn't it? The wood is just as strikingly beautiful. The legs run all the way through from the top of the cabinet to the floor, just like the one above. But this one looks more elegant, more delicate and more formal. Not any better, just different. It's these elements used in different ways that make furniture what it is — a personal statement of the craftsman who made it.

This midsize cabinet is a mixture of several ideas. It has the feel of a dry sink, but has two drawers instead of the box for the pitcher and face bowl. The doors have brightly colored panels that contrast with the cabinet wood and complement the four turned knobs. The drawers have chiseled oval recesses that retain the tool marks. The design elements were carefully chosen to fit with one another. The result is a somewhat whimsical but useful piece of furniture.

Sometimes it's fun to create something a little different. While looking through a catalog of contemporary furniture, I saw a chest of drawers that was wide at the top and tapered to a narrow base. Its appearance was striking. I accidentally turned the catalog upside down and it hit me. Build the chest wide at the bottom, tapering to a narrow top. I added the removable jewelry box so that the top of the chest wouldn't seem to stop so abruptly. With the addition of the small box echoing the larger chest, the whole unit seems content and complete.

DRESSERS

PHOTO BELOW Meet the Chester County tall chest. This is a solid-looking and exquisite chest of drawers. The raised panels on the sides, the three arched top drawers, the moulding under the top and the choice of curly maple make this chest what it is. Picture the sides as solid panels, the legs square and straight, the edges of the top square, no moulding under the top, and straight-grained mahogany or pine. What if the chest was painted? These elements determine how a piece looks and feels, and what kind of personality it has.

ABOVE PHOTO When it comes to simplicity of design and practicality of usage, the Shakers knew what they were doing. This chest of drawers was designed from a photo of an original piece. The original was made of plain-sliced maple, with curly maple for the drawer fronts. This version was made of quartersawn sycamore. By carefully looking at the grain patterns and arranging them in a pleasing pattern, the furniture maker allowed the wood to have a direct say in how this piece was finished and presented. The light-colored wood makes this piece less overwhelming. It is 20"-deep by 42"-wide by 64"-tall. These six drawers provide a tremendous amount of space.

Here's a Shaker press cupboard. The cabinet was originally made with solid-paneled doors, but with glass doors it becomes a showcase cabinet. This piece is deceptive in its seemingly simple design. The top moulding is simple and straight, as is the upper cabinet. But at the base of the upper cabinet is a cove moulding that cleverly blends the upper unit with the lower table. The table becomes a base that has a large drawer, a square-edged top, and legs that start out square at the top but are turned all the way to the floor. The doors have a wooden latching mechanism that keeps the feel of the piece more handmade than would a metal latch. Once again, the choice of wood is not something to be overlooked.

Make no mistake about it, this Townsend Newport high chest reveals plenty about the craftsman who built it. The legs, scrollwork and single finial make a bold statement. Having these features at the base of this chest tells us that the rest of this cabinet is also top-quality construction. After all, isn't the working section supported by the best visual and technical aspects of the whole piece? Note the cove moulding at the top and bottom of the upper drawer section. The drawers have hand-cut dovetails and solid-wood bottoms. Would you expect anything else after seeing the outside of this piece? The style of this piece makes it a specialty item. It could work as a stand-alone piece, but it commands a lot of attention, so if it is placed in a room with other furniture it must be complemented by equally strong pieces.

SIDEBOARDS AND HUTCHES

The flexibility of this Shaker tailor's cabinet is what makes it a good piece for any room in the house. The drop leaf is an option; if you want a little more area on the top for a larger project, you've got it. The original was made of plain and figured maple. The turned feet help soften the look of this cabinet, but it would work just as well with square feet. The trademark feature on all Shaker cabinetry is the turned knobs. They are easy to grasp for opening and closing the drawers and doors.

This John Seymour sideboard has straight lines, a square-edged top, gently tapering legs, two drawers, two doors and tambour doors. So what makes this piece what it is? Its flat surfaces provide a palette for the craftsman. He inlaid veneers of several species of wood into simple but effective shapes. The top is marble, which brings yet another natural element into this piece. It's interesting to see how the material from several different trees and a large piece of rock can be harvested, refined, worked and joined together, yet retain their individual characteristics. In our time, we have access to all the tools, plans and materials needed to create these pieces. One thing that hasn't changed is time. We all wish we had more! A piece like this is doable, but it does take planning, gathering and building — which take time.

This hutch design is based on a Kentucky style of building reminiscent of the Shakers. The lines are smooth and mostly straight. The subtle raised panels on the base cabinet don't conflict with the flat-panel glass doors. The scrollwork on the front base apron and sides connects all of the legs in a pleasing line that continues through the legs to the floor. The use of glass in furniture can make a big difference. Try to picture this hutch with solid-wood panels in the upper doors. It would still look great, but being able to see into the hutch adds depth and makes it look lighter.

One stand out feature of this Pennsylvania stepback cupboard is the hinges. They add an almost whimsical feel. This plain design is modified with lightly scalloped upper face-frame stiles and boldly scalloped feet. The addition of the through-dovetails on the feet complements the bold look of the hinges. The top cove moulding has beading at the bottom, and the rounded edge of the top complements that moulding nicely. The glass doors make this a wonderful display cabinet.

If you keep the dimensions on a corner hutch small, a well-proportioned cabinet is the result. A corner cabinet can become too wide very quickly when the depth is increased. The scrollwork on this cabinet is kept to a minimum because the strong grain of the stained oak does all the talking. This cabinet has a more casual look and feel with the self-closing hinges that mount on the face frame, as well as the porcelain knobs and pulls. With different hardware and wood, this hutch would look more formal. One interesting feature is the ledge rail on the top of the cabinet. It finishes the top of the hutch without using traditional moulding.

This Shaker stepback is a reproduction of an original piece. The five-step crown moulding, the row of drawers in the top section, the scrollwork on the base, and the painted finish make this piece interesting. One very important design element is how a piece is finished. This is a good example of how paint can be just as effective as leaving the wood exposed.

Office file storage doesn't need to be a boring metal file cabinet. This curly maple filing cabinet is both functional and stylish. The three doors (two with glass), open shelves and angled feet are arranged to create a nonsymmetrical look that breaks up the narrow and tall look of the cabinet. A lot of storage is contained in a small amount of floor space.

This versatile walnut sideboard could be used in a dining room, entertainment room or bedroom. The style is simple and unadorned. The choice of hardware or the type of wood would determine the function of this cabinet as much as where it was placed. The hardware on the feet complements the exposed screw heads on the doorknobs. The lion's-head pulls may not be original to the piece, but they make a rather strong statement on an otherwise subdued cabinet.

chapter 8

FREESTANDING AND BUILT-IN

bookcases
and media centers

Bookcases are cabinets with shelves that hold heavy loads. **Media centers**

house televisions and tons of electronic equipment. Both types of cabinets need to

be **sturdy** and still look **stylish**.

screws, so it can be disassembled in a few minutes, moved and reassembled very easily.

I chose red oak for the cabinet because I wanted the bookcase to have a strong, solid look and feel. The oak was stained a dark walnut color to further show the strong character of its grain. The raised panels are made of African mahogany, which gives the bookcase a slightly formal look and adds a nice contrasting color to the oak.

I wanted the bookcase to have a lighter look, so I built it with a ½"-thick plywood back and made the base with legs. This gives the bookcase a floating look and doesn't anchor it visually to the floor like a solid base with mouldings would do.

I designed it for an older home that has 8"-high base mouldings in its rooms. The legs are set in 1" from the back of the cabinet

FREESTANDING BOOKCASES

The bookcase on page 58 is about 7' tall and 4' wide. I wanted this bookcase to be an individual piece of furniture that could be moved to wherever it would look and function best. It is made of two side panels, one center panel, a bottom and a top, a base, a top crown moulding assembly, a back and shelves. The whole cabinet is held together with

so it will clear the base moulding and can be pushed tightly against the wall. I mounted the front legs at an angle, to add visual movement to the piece. I glued and screwed the base together using butt joints and plugged the screw holes with contrasting wooden plugs, which added another visual element.

As book shelves are filled, the weight is transferred to the sides and down to the floor. I inset the end legs about an inch

The base gives this bookcase a lighter look and also allows the unit to be pushed tightly against the wall. Note the plugged screw holes. This is another visual design element that gives a hint as to how the base is assembled.

As you can see here, the shelves have been set back so the front edge of the shelves meets the back side of the cove on the front edges of the side and center panels. This adds visual movement to the front of the bookcase. The sides are $1\frac{1}{8}$" thick, but are made to look thinner by coves routed on both sides of the front edges. This detail is repeated on the shelves and the bottom panel.

but made sure they were still under the sides so the weight of the bookcase would be transferred from the sides down through the legs to the floor. The legs in the center of the base add to the solidity of the unit by transferring the center divider's weight to the floor. Without this set of legs, the bookcase would sag in the middle of the bottom panel, and eventually the bookcase would weaken from the stress.

The sides of a cabinet need to be supported or made of strong material that will maintain its rigidity. If the sides are not supported, the weight of the books will cause the sides to bend outward. I've seen shelves fall because the sides of the bookcase bent so much that even the length of the shelf pins wasn't enough to keep the shelves in place.

The side and center panels in this bookcase are made of $1\frac{1}{8}$"-thick oak and are very strong. The sides of bookcases can be made from $\frac{3}{4}$" plywood. These

panels should be strengthened by attaching solid-wood strips (usually $\frac{3}{4}$" × $1\frac{1}{4}$" or $1\frac{1}{2}$") to the front edges. If the bookcase is built-in, these front-edge strips can serve as fitting strips.

The shelves in a bookcase need to be strong. If they are made longer than 30" they need to be supported along their lengths. This bookcase has solid oak shelves 1"-thick by 22"-long. They will never sag! Shelves made with $\frac{3}{4}$" plywood and solid-wood edging ($\frac{3}{4}$" × $1\frac{1}{4}$" or $1\frac{1}{2}$") are strong and economical.

A profile can be routed in the hardwood edges to make them more decorative. When I built this bookcase I had one router bit and a $\frac{1}{2}$" core-box bit which I used to create all the profiles on the bookcase. The material for the sides and the base legs is thick for strength, but I wanted a physically lighter look so I routed coves on both sides of all the front edges of the side panels, center panel, base legs and shelves. These edges could have been beveled to 45° on both sides to achieve the same effect.

For a neater and cleaner look, the

This simple crown moulding is made by cutting two parallel grooves in the top moulding strips. The same
core-box bit used elsewhere on this bookcase was used to create these grooves.

bookcase facts

- Shelves should be 10" deep. This will accommodate books of nearly any size.
- Shelves should be no longer than 30" without vertical supports along their lengths.
- Shelves should be ¾"- to 1"-thick solid wood or be made of ¾" plywood with a ¾" × 1½" solid-wood strip attached to the front edge of the shelf.
- Freestanding bookcases should have at least ½"-thick plywood backs — ¾" if the bookcase is large. This will add tremendous strength to the entire cabinet and help hold it square.

shelf-pin holes are 5mm in diameter. These are smaller than ¼"-diameter shelf-pin holes and are not as obtrusive. For an even cleaner look, I chose to use shelf pins that disappear into a groove machined into the ends of the shelves. When the shelves are in place they have no visible means of support: They look like they are floating in the cabinet.

The crown moulding is made with two ½" flutes routed along its length. These flutes echo the coves on the front edges of the bookcase. By adding moulding to the top of the bookcase I created a visual line that carries your eye past the top of the sides and cabinet. Your eye follows the moulding outward along its lines and adds a smooth transition to the very top of the bookcase.

These sides have raised panels made with a core-box router bit. That same bit
is used to rout a cove on the inside edges of the side's frame.

make knockdown cabinets using screws

I've built a lot of casework that is assembled with screws. It's a simple, easy and strong way to build cabinetry — especially large cabinets that cannot be moved easily or cannot be brought into a room fully assembled. The major components that make up a basic cabinet are the sides, bottom, rails, back, base, top, drawers and doors.

- Rabbets are cut into the back edges of the side panels. The backs of the cabinets are installed with screws driven into the rabbets.
- If the cabinet has front rails and/or drawer rails, pocket holes can be drilled into the ends of the rails. The rails are then butted up to the sides and attached with screws driven into the pocket holes.
- Bottoms can be attached the same way as the rails, to the inside of the side panels with pocket holes and screws. Another method is to cut rabbets into the bottoms of the sides and set the bottom panel into the rabbets with screws. Depending on the design of the cabinet, the bottom panel can be attached directly to the bottom of the side panel with screws driven up through the bottom panel.
- Tops can be attached to the tops of the side panels by screwing through cleats attached to the top inside edges of the side panels. Or pocket holes could be drilled into the top inside edges of the sides.
- Doors can be attached using clip-on European-style hinges. The hinge plate stays attached to the cabinet side, and the hinge stays attached to the door. When the cabinet has been assembled, clip the doors into place.
- Drawers can be mounted using metal slides. One part of the slide is mounted on the cabinet side, and the other part is mounted on the drawer. Simply slide the drawer into place — it's that easy!
- If all the cabinet parts are made to be knockdown, it is much easier to finish the parts while the cabinet is disassembled.

This Arts & Crafts knockdown bookshelf is very practical. The through mortise-and-tenon joints with the wedges are extremely strong. The bookshelf has no back, so the wall color will show through, helping it blend into any room.

BUILT-IN BOOKCASES

BUILT-IN BOOKCASES CAN ADD an elegant look, feel and functionality to a room. If the room is fairly large (15' × 20' and larger), built-ins that go from floor to ceiling would be a good choice.

Bookcases built floor to ceiling create a library-like feel. If you have a lot of books, this is the way to go. Another choice is to build base cabinets that are 24" to 30" high and 15" to 20" deep. (See photos at right.)

These base cabinets can have traditional hinged doors, sliding doors or no doors. Bookcases can be built on top of the base cabinets. This entire unit can be built between two walls or built into a corner with one finished end and the other fitted to a wall. This base cabinet/bookcase arrangement offers a lot of storage space.

The choice of finish for built-in bookcase units can make a lot of difference in a room. If the units are painted the same or a similar color as the room, they will blend into the room nicely. If the units are made of richly colored or grained wood and left natural or stained, they add a feeling of elegance and warmth to the room.

Built-in bookcase units are usually finished at the bottom with base moulding and at the top with crown moulding, adding a feeling of permanence and solidity to the room.

Built-in bookcases can be fit around doorways, windows and fireplaces. If it's built around windows, a nice touch is a window seat, which would connect the two cabinets on either side of the window. The seat could even double as a lidded storage box.

Built-in bookcases and shelving can be made to look solid and stately by adding fluted columns and staining the knotty pine wood dark. Note the lights mounted in the slightly arched top. The shelves in the lower photo were later changed to wooden frame, tempered glass shelves so that the light could shine through to the base cabinet top. The base moulding was built to match existing base moulding used throughout the house. Base cabinets built below bookcases or open shelving can add a lot of storage space to a room. This one has traditional swinging doors, but sliding doors would also be an excellent option. This whole unit filled a 12' wall at one end of a 25'-long room. It blended into the room nicely.

When building bookcases into a room, remember that you will lose some square footage in the room — not much, but this could give a small room the feeling of being "closed in." Dark paint on the cabinets or dark woods will also make the room feel smaller.

One option to help a room keep its open feeling is to build the bookcases 6" to 12" from the ceiling. Then mount recessed lights on top of the bookcases. This will indirectly light the room and add a warm and spacious feeling.

Another option is to build the bookcases without backs. After the bookcases are installed, they will be very sturdy. The color of the walls will show through and make the shelving appear lighter — even after books and knickknacks are added.

If the built-in bookcases are more for decoration than for books, a tempered glass shelf or a wooden frame with tempered glass mounted in it can be used to lighten the look of the shelving. If lights are mounted in the tops of the bookcases to shine down through the shelving, the effect is quite dramatic.

Other features, such as arching the inside tops of the bookcases or adding fluting to the fronts of the sides and dividers, add nice visual touches to the overall look and feel of the built-ins. Fluted edges combined with a base and/or top plinth can make built-ins appear stately.

DOORS

Doors can be added to built-in bookcases if the shelves need to be hidden or the books need to be protected. Doors with glass panels are less obtrusive than solid doors but offer less protection from ultra-

violet light and direct sunlight. Obviously, both will protect the books from dust and unwanted hands. If doors are needed, be sure to take into account the fact that they need room to open. Make sure window and door casings don't interfere with the operation of the bookcase doors.

Another option is sliding doors. They need no space to open into a room, but require a deeper cabinet so they can be mounted in tracks. Both glass and solid doors can be used as sliding doors. A door with glass mounted in a wooden frame makes a nice sliding door.

This unit is made of poplar that has a cherry stain applied to it. The effect is wonderful. The arch at the top of the bookcase and the appliqué on the face of the header add a touch of elegance. The appliqué on the top header can be purchased at any woodworking supply store (see suppliers list on page 127).

When permanently installing cabinets, be sure to check all heating and cooling ductwork and electrical outlets. Before this shelving and storage unit could be installed, a heating unit had to be blocked off and an electrical outlet was moved higher so it was accessible. The top moulding was built to match existing door and window mouldings in the rest of the house, and the cabinet was painted to match the walls. A natural or stained wood cabinet would have competed for attention with other furnishings in the room. This is an excellent example of how a built-in cabinet can blend seamlessly into the walls of a room.

A third option is tambour doors. They don't open into the room, but they do require a deeper cabinet than just front-mounted sliding doors. The tracks for tambour doors take up room at the front, sides and back of the shelf unit. These types of doors can add a nice, clean-line look to the bookcases.

A fourth option is retractable doors — doors that swing on hinges to 90° and then are pushed into pockets at the sides of the cabinet. This gives the swing-open door the ability to slide out of the way. These doors require 2" to 5" on each side of the cabinet, and additional vertical shelf supports are needed for the shelves. Hardware available for this type of door has slides that are mounted on the insides of the cabinet and hinges that are mounted to the slides. Another way to make this door is to cut tracks on the inside of the top and bottom of the cabinet, attach pins at the top and bottom of the door, and set the pins to glide in the tracks in the cabinet. The pins act as hinge, glide and slide.

MEDIA CENTERS

MEDIA AND ENTERTAINMENT centers have become common in most households that have a television, stereo system, CD player, DVD player and, in some cases, a large-screen television.

Media centers can take several shapes and sizes, depending on their intended uses: How many electronic components will be housed in the cabinet? Will it be in a bedroom, living room or den?

The cabinet above is made specifically to house an integrated amplifier, CD player and a turntable. A pullout drawer holds CDs, and the lower sections hold records. It fits well in a living room.

The design is based on the simple and straight lines of Shaker furniture with the addition of contrasting colored panels for the doors. The cabinet is rectangular, but the four legs flare from top to bottom. This adds some subtle visual movement to an otherwise rectilinear cabinet.

The cabinet is made of unstained cherry with padauk door panels. As the cherry and padauk age, the colors will blend nicely with one another. If the cherry had been stained, it would have changed color anyway. This would create a very dark color that would not have enough contrast with the deep burgundy color of the padauk.

Sometimes all you need is a base corner cabinet that a television can sit on. The cabinet could be used to hold videotapes and CDs. Also, a video or DVD player could be housed in the base cabinet. This type of cabinet is good when space is at a premium or where a smaller cabinet is preferred. This type of setup is unobtrusive and creates a formal stand for the television.

This entertainment center houses audio components only. It is in a room that is fairly sparse in its decor, so the Shaker-influenced cabinet was a good choice. All the wires and cables are fed down a chase in the left-hand rear corner of the cabinet and come out under the unit. The plugs are then plugged into a power strip and the speaker wires are easily hooked up to remote speakers in the room.

LARGE MEDIA CENTERS

A couple came to me looking for a cabinet that would house their five separate electronic components: two large speakers, television, CD collection, videotapes, records and a lot of their children's toys! They had a fairly large room (14' × 20'), so a large cabinet was not going to dwarf the rest of the room. The freestanding cabinet was to have a simple but formal look and be stained to match other pieces of furniture in the room.

It became a sugar pine cabinet with raised-panel doors and crown moulding. It measured 25"-deep by 84"-high by 96"-wide. I decided to make a base and upper unit that could be separated from one another.

The center of the top section was to house the television. The two center doors needed to retract into the cabinet when they were open so the television could be viewed from any location in the room. Pocket-door hardware to make this type of door is available from many woodworking and cabinetmaking suppliers. (See suppliers list on page 127.) The two center doors in the lower cabinet match the upper doors. This center section in the lower cabinet has three draw-

The upper center section of this media center houses the television. The shelf above the television holds the video and DVD players. The lower section has an open shelf for future video components and two drawers to hold videotapes and DVDs.

ers for videotapes and CDs.

When constructing cabinets that will hold televisions, be sure to take into account the weight of the television. The weight can make an unsupported shelf sag or fail. Your design could include a lower cabinet with a partition under the center of the television cabinet. That would support a very heavy television indeed!

Televisions can be mounted on pullout shelves that also swivel. This is a nice feature if the room has several different viewing locations. The pullout/swivel

hardware is available from most woodworking and cabinetmaking suppliers. (See list of suppliers on page 127.)

One area in many newer homes that is great for built-in cabinets, bookcases or a media center, is around fireplaces. Most builders don't furnish cabinetry that can be put beside fireplaces. The owners have to go to a custom cabinetmaker to get what they want.

Many newer fireplaces have hearths that are 6" to 24" in height, and project out from the wall 14" to 24". Most have

This entertainment center was designed to be used as a television cabinet, as a music center (with all of the components as well as the speakers in the cabinet), and as storage for records, CDs, DVDs, videos and lots of toys! It makes a nice piece of furniture for a fairly large room.

This large media center is built in six sections: three upper cabinets and three lower cabinets. The center section is 28" deep because the television that is to go into the cabinet in the future is large. The side base cabinets are 24" deep, and the upper side cabinets are 12" deep. The whole unit is 8' tall and almost 10' wide. By varying the depths of the cabinets and having the upper side cabinets open, I was able to diminish the massive look of the unit. The choice of natural mahogany wood was a compromise. The client wanted a dark wood, but I suggested that a medium-colored wood would help lighten the look and mass of the unit. The client agreed, and the unit still retained a good, rich wood color with nice grain patterns.

media center facts

- Cabinets that house televisions need to be at least 24" to 26" deep. Take this into account when planning where the cabinet will sit or be installed. Measure the television that will be going into the cabinet to be absolutely sure of the cabinet depth. Remember to include the thickness of the doors and the back of the cabinet.
- Always measure every piece of electronic equipment that will be going into a media center before you cut any materials!
- Inserts that fit into drawers and hold DVDs, CDs, videocassettes and audiocassettes are the best way to store these items. These inserts can be purchased from most woodworking and cabinetmaking suppliers (see suppliers list on page 127). For those of you who want to build your own drawer dividers, here are the specifications:

	T	W	H
CDs	$7/16$"	$4^{15}/16$"	$5^5/8$"
DVDs	$5/8$"	$5^3/8$"	$7^1/2$"
VIDEOTAPES	1"	$7^9/16$"	$4^1/8$"
RECORD ALBUMS	$3/16$"	$12^3/8$"	$12^3/8$"
AUDIOCASSETTES	$11/16$"	$4^5/16$"	$2^3/4$"

The barrister-style bookcase seems to never go out of style. Each case is built as an individual box with a garage-type glass door. You can build as many as you need now and add more later. These look good made of stained oak or, as shown here, cherry.

brick hearths. The border around the opening is also brick, and the mantel is an inexpensive wooden shelf. This type of configuration is usually on one blank wall. Building base cabinets the same depth as the hearth and 20" to 30" high, with bookcases above them, is a nice way to utilize this space. Base cabinets and bookcases on either side of the fireplace provide plenty of storage space for games, toys, electronic equipment and a picture to be hung above the fireplace.

The base cabinets could house video and audio equipment, and a television could be set on top of the cabinet. Some people prefer the television to be housed in the base cabinet, however. Drawers can be hidden behind doors in the base cabinets for storing videos and audiotapes, CDs and DVDs.

I once made a set of fireplace surround cabinets that had sliding doors on the base cabinets, which housed an audio system. There were wooden-frame glass sliding doors on the upper cabinets, which held a wonderful collection of books that looked very nice on the wall in the client's family room!

Another client wanted 24"-deep base cabinets and 15"-deep bookcases on top.

Top moulding will run the full length of multiple cabinets.

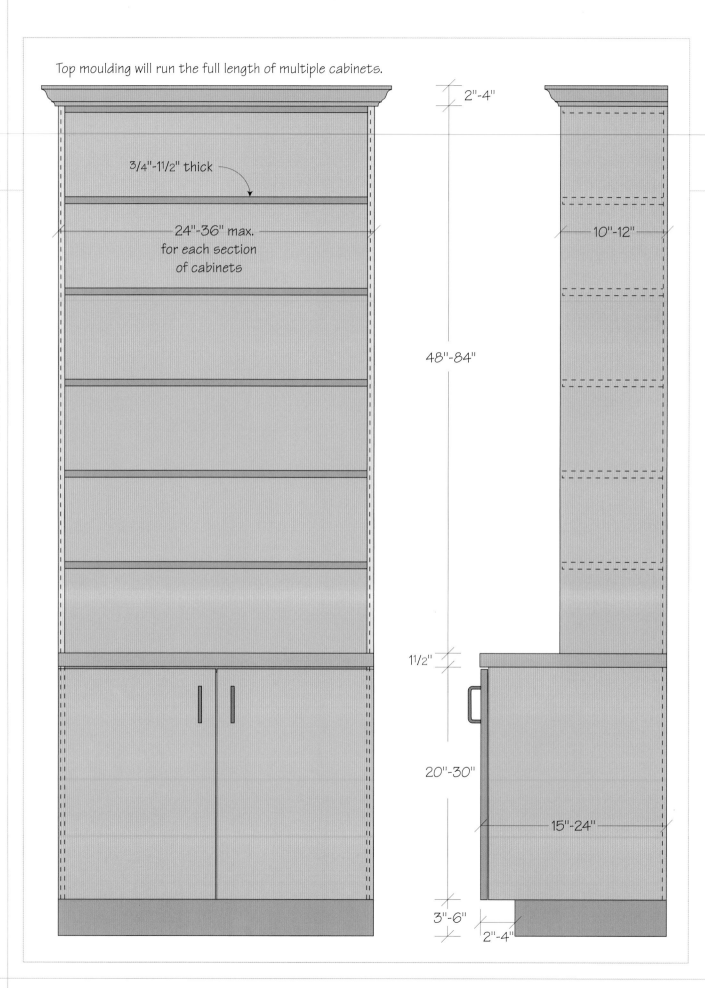

3/4"-1½" thick

24"-36" max.
for each section
of cabinets

2"-4"

10"-12"

48"-84"

11/2"

20"-30"

15"-24"

3"-6"

2"-4"

cabinet depth

As a general rule, cabinets that are deeper than 24" will make a room feel smaller. They actually take 2' from the space of the room. This is sometimes hard to visualize, and only when the cabinets have been built and installed do people realize they've "boxed" themselves into a room. If a room is to become a den or library and bookcases are wanted all around the room, they should not be any deeper than 12". As stated earlier in this chapter, 10"-deep bookcases will hold all but the largest books.

This Chippendale linen press cabinet could be used as an armoire or a media center. The curly maple in this piece is used beautifully; the grain patterns have been matched to complement each other, creating a visual treat. The style of the piece is fairly simple. The ogee feet, the quarter-round columns at the front corners and the crown moulding at the top combine nicely to create a piece that is well balanced.

Above the fireplace they wanted the wall paneled the same as the cabinets, and two 12"-deep open shelves between the bookcases. The client had some trophies to display on these open shelves.

I've also built a surround cabinet with can lights (recessed flush-mounted lights) installed in the top of the upper cabinet to illuminate a porcelain collection. A television housed in the base cabinet was mounted on a pullout/swivel shelf.

Here's an idea for those of you who have a little more means: I once made a set of wall-to-wall base cabinets that spanned about 18'. The television was housed in the center of this base unit. It sat on a shelf that was elevated straight up out of the cabinet by an electric motor operated by remote control. When the television was not in use it was lowered until it disappeared back into the cabinet. The top of the television shelf unit was then flush with the top of the base cabinet and blended in perfectly with the rest of the cabinet. Bookcases were built to the ceiling on top of the base cabinets, on either side of the television base cabinet. The bookcases were finished at the ceiling with crown moulding. The wall of cabinets was then filled with law books and made a striking addition to the room.

Large-screen televisions usually sit on the floor, and cabinets are then built around them. These cabinets are usually 28" to 32" deep and over 4' tall. If you want to house one of these televisions, make sure the room is large enough to handle the space needed.

chapter 9

tables

The family gathers around the **kitchen table**, treasured art books are displayed

on the **coffee table**, keys are tossed on the **hall table**. Tables put people and

their possessions **within reach** and won't complain about how long they might

need to hold these **precious gifts** for us.

This is a Queen Anne drop-leaf table. The left and right legs pivot inward, allowing the two leaves to fold down. If necessary, the table could be pushed against a wall and used easily by two people, with the option of adding another seat by simply folding up one leaf. Four people can sit at this table comfortably and have lots of leg room. The round top creates a more intimate feel than would a square tabletop of the same size.

TABLES

A table is a horizontal surface supported by a base. Its function is to supply a surface to hold all kinds of things: papers, books, lamps, dishes, boxes.

And there are all kinds of tables: dining, nightstands, lamp, coffee, end, sofa, hall, plant stands, picnic, lab, folding — the list goes on.

Tables traditionally have four legs and a top. The legs are held together with aprons forming the table base. The top is attached to the base with screws, metal angle brackets, bolts, wooden brackets, sliding dovetail slots, or cleats.

These are the basic parts. How all of the parts fit together, and in what style and shape, is where the designing starts.

The shape of the legs can determine how the table will actually appear to sit on the floor. Straight, square legs are easy to make and have worked well for thousands of years. If the legs are slim, the rest of the table should be visually light. If a stronger or more solid look is wanted, the top could be made thicker or it could have a larger overhang, past the legs and apron — or both.

If the legs are made thicker, from 2" to 8" square, a dramatic change takes place. The table demands attention and almost shows off its strength. In a large room, this can be effective and put to good use. You can place large centerpieces and candles on these tables with no fear of overwhelming either the table or the room.

MAKING TABLETOPS LARGER

One clever idea to make a top larger, when it is needed, is to have leaves that are hinged to the main top. They are folded down when not needed, then lifted up and supported by braces when extra table space is needed.

The practice of making removable leaves is also a brilliant idea (or maybe I'm just easily impressed). Depending on how large the slides are between the two halves of the tabletop, a 4' square table can be extended up to 12' long. Leaves laid between the tabletop halves and resting on the slides enlarge the top surface.

In the case of tables extending more than 8', a fifth leg is added in the middle. This extra leg is attached to the table's slides and nests between the other legs when the leaf is not in use. As the table is opened, the leg rides along on the underside of the slides. Another type of center leg can fold up under the table and drop down as needed.

Tabletops can also be made larger by the use of leaves that slide under the tabletop. These leaves run on slides that are offset, so that the leaf can be pulled out and raised flush with the tabletop.

Some tables have multilayered tops, one top cantilevering under another, pivoting on pins at their corners and fanning out like a deck of cards in a magician's hands.

A square table can be made round by adding to each edge a fold-up leaf that is straight on the back and curved on the front. When the four leaves are folded out, their curves form a circle.

This conference table has two cylinders for legs, and the top freely spans the space between them. The room is not large, so putting traditional legs under the top would have made access awkward. Clients can simply sit down and roll their chairs comfortably up to the table.

This small kitchen table and chairs were designed to have a light visual look. The chairs' and table's legs are painted a dark green, which helps draw attention to the light mahogany seats and tabletop. The two folding leaves form a round table when they are raised into position. When they are dropped, the table can be pushed against a wall to gain some space in the rest of the kitchen.

table facts

- Nightstands are 24" to 30" high.
- Sofa or hall tables are 26" to 32" high.
- For every person sitting at a table, allow no less than 24" of width. For good elbow room 26" to 30" is much better.
- On a table with a solid base in the middle, allow at least 12" for knee room from the outside edge of the tabletop to the base. But 14" to 15" is much better if you can manage it without the table becoming unstable.
- On dining tables with legs and aprons, the height from the floor to the bottom of the apron should be 24" to 25".

- Round tables will seat more people than a same-size square table. What you don't get is more space in the middle, so use a lazy Susan!
- Tables with three legs will sit on any uneven surface without rocking.
- Whenever a glass tabletop or a glass shelf is used, the glass must be tempered. There can be no exceptions to this. A tempered piece of glass is much stronger than untempered glass. An untempered piece of glass, if broken, will shatter into shards that can cause serious bodily harm. A tempered piece of glass, if broken, will crumble into gravel-sized pieces that are not as likely to cause any serious injury.

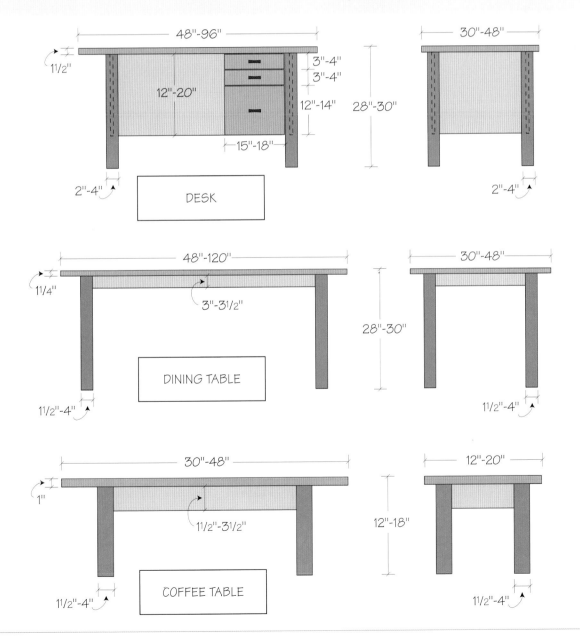

DESK

DINING TABLE

COFFEE TABLE

TOP SHAPES

A table can have a curved front and a straight back that fits against a wall. This is a nice look for a hall table or small telephone or message table. A tabletop with a square corner and a curved front will fit easily into a corner and become a lamp holder or flower stand.

Round tables work well in the middle of a room. A round tabletop can serve as a place for people to sit and play cards or board games, talk or dine. The round table shape makes for a more intimate setting because all who sit around the table are equal at their places. There is no head or side to the table.

A conference table usually seats ten or more people. Its shape creates territories for those seated at the table. A rectangular table has two sides and two heads. The people at the heads are usually in control of the meeting. The shape of the table puts the focus on them. A conference table that has curved sides and squared ends serves the same purpose.

A conference table that is shaped like a racetrack is a more subtle approach to the "who's in charge" idea. The sides are straight but the ends are curved, so two or three people can sit at the heads of the table and no one person is the focus.

Some conference tables are round. Worldwide summit meetings often use round tables, sometimes 20' to 30' in diameter. This puts all sitting at the

The base of this coffee table started out as one piece, but it seemed a little *too* rooted to the floor. When it was split, it still held its ground, but did so with finesse. And as a plus, cats love the space between the base pieces.

Wrought iron and tile were used to make this table and chairs. This set adds a cheery feel to the kitchen and it will last forever.

conference table on equal footing.

Some conference tables are shaped like the capital letter D. These tables put the focus on the individuals who sit on the straight side, but these people do not have control of the meeting, because the indi-

This coffee table serves double duty. If the leaves are folded down, as shown, the table has an elegant oval appearance. The leaves can also be folded up at a 90° angle to form a box, and the top becomes a butler tray which can be lifted off of the base and carried away.

viduals on the curved side almost surround those on the straight side. These tables are good for questioning or interrogating individuals. The blackjack tables at casinos are also D-shaped, so that the dealer is the focus and has all the control, while all who are playing the game are gathered around this central figure. Also, these tables are tall. The players could stand (and sometimes do) but seats are provided for them to sit, stay and play. The dealer remains standing throughout the game, thus gaining even more control of the table.

If you want to have a more competitive game of cards, try sitting at a square table as opposed to a round table. See what happens when each player has his own side!

Hexagonal or octagonal tables, with their flattened edges, set up separate places for those sitting at the table.

A rectangular dining table has a place for the father and mother at the heads and the children on the sides, joining the family together as a unit. The feelings generated by a table having these areas of separation are real. How often does one go to someone's house and sit at the head of the table unless asked to do so?

TABLE BASES

The configuration of the base of a table is as important as the shape of the tabletop. As stated earlier, tables usually have legs rather than a solid base. The reason is simple: A table that is to be used by people, especially if they are seated at the table, needs to have room under the top for the chairs and the people's legs.

There is one kind of table that doesn't have legs for a base. It's called a box table because it's just that, a box. These are commonly used as lamp tables, nightstands or for any application that doesn't require the table to be used for seating.

To give this tabletop a floating look, it was built so that the legs don't actually touch the top. The side aprons and two stringers linking the aprons support the top instead. Note that the end aprons are located lower than the side aprons. This makes it possible to add another visual element to the table and cut longer tenons on all the aprons.

Sometimes, table legs can get in the way of people's feet and legs. A center support column with feet that are attached very low on the column is a good way to create more leg room. On longer tables, this column can become a trestle. A trestle is made with two end panels connected by a stringer. A tabletop is then placed on this assembly. The end panels can be shaped with cutouts to form feet, and the stringer can be attached to the panels with through-tenons. Removable pins can fix the stringer in place.

Cylinders can be used as a base for a table. These usually look best with a round tabletop. Remember that knee space is required (12" to 14" from the edge of the table to the outside of the base). The larger diameter the top and the larger the base, the more stable the table.

A mushroom-shaped base (larger at the bottom and tapering to the top) creates a striking table that was popular in the late 1950s and early 1960s. This style of table is stable and offers more than enough knee and leg room.

A waterfall table is shaped like a flattened, inverted U. One leg is vertical from the floor, curves 90° to form the top, then descends 90° again to form the opposite leg. These tables are solid and can function as coffee tables right on up to dining tables. Obviously, seating at these dining tables is on the sides only!

The Parsons table is sleek looking and has straight lines throughout. The legs and the aprons are all the same dimension; for example, if the legs are 3" square, then the aprons are 3" thick. This is another one of those styles that work for everything from small coffee tables to

Walnut veneer was used in a starburst pattern to create the design for this coffee table. The pattern is bookmatched on the top and the cone base. Getting the veneer to match and wrap around the base was a great challenge! The results exceeded my expectations.

The round, stained, burled maple inlay was also created in a starburst pattern to match the seam lines of the walnut veneer.

Based on the Parsons table design, this coffee table is made of ash and finished with black lacquer. It has a formal look but could be used in a variety of settings.

dining tables and from square lamp tables to long and sleek hall or sofa tables.

If a Parsons table is made of solid wood, a nice touch is to create a double-miter joint where the side apron, end apron and leg meet. A veneered top can be set into the framework of the side and end aprons. The edges on a Parsons table are usually left fairly square, but a $\frac{1}{4}$" to $\frac{1}{2}$" roundover on all edges adds a nice softening effect that makes the table more user-friendly, especially on shorter coffee tables.

To add a more Oriental feel to a Parsons table, the legs can have feet that turn inward. This gives the visual effect of the table "bowing down" or "kneeling."

Running a bead around all the edges of a Parsons table gives the table a less sleek look, adds another layer of depth and softens the feel.

I've made Parsons tables in two halves connected with slides that allowed the table to be pulled apart so leaves could be added.

A nice effect is making a table base that supports a glass top. Glass tops lighten the look of any table and therefore work well in a small space. Note: Whenever a glass tabletop or a glass shelf is used, the glass must be tempered. There can be no exceptions to this. An untempered piece of glass, if broken, will shatter into shards that can cause serious bodily harm. A tempered piece of glass, if broken, will crumble into gravel-sized pieces that are not as likely to cause any serious injury. Also, a tempered piece of glass is much stronger than untempered glass.

Sometimes you need to have some fun. This table is made of laminated strips of wood, and the redheart wood in the center of the laminations is a real visual treat for the eye.

The Mount Lebanon Shaker counter is a unique piece of furniture. It has a great work surface for everything from baking to sewing, and the drawers provide an incredible amount of storage space. This table is 28"-deep by 35"-high by 72"-long. The figured maple drawer fronts contrast with and complement the walnut sides, legs and top. The ebonized drawer pulls add a crispness to the drawer fronts.

This end table has legs curved in just one plane, but they were set at a 45° angle to the aprons, which makes the legs look like they curve in two planes. After looking at the table for a while, your eye will pick up on the trick, but it is fun nonetheless. To further draw the eye to the nontraditional configuration of the legs, the top's corners were clipped at a 45° angle and beveled. This makes the legs appear to extend up into the corner of the top. This was one of those last-minute things that pulled the whole table together.

This dining table is also based on the Parsons table style. The legs and aprons are all 4" square. This particular table is made of ash and is lacquered gloss black. The strong grain of the ash can be seen in its texture. The black color gives the table a formal appearance in any setting. Adding the tempered glass top gives the whole table a sleek and formal appearance since it doesn't look as large as it actually is. Six people can sit comfortably around this table.

Here's a simple but sturdy tavern table. The tapered legs and the breadboard ends on the top make this table distinctive. Painting the base dark draws your eye to the lighter top, which is a rich-colored wood.

This is a formal dining table in the Queen Anne style. It has a veneered top and veneered aprons, but the carved edges on the top and the carving on the legs are the highlights of this piece!

This Stickley side table contrasts sharply with the dining table above, but it has its own elegant appeal. The clipped corners on the top, the panels connecting the aprons and the curved stretchers, and the quarter-sawn white oak make this piece what it is — a sturdy but visually light table. It would work in any room of the house.

Round tables can seat several people at one time. This table has three legs because it was designed to go in locations where the floor would not always be flat and level. A three-legged table or chair will sit on any uneven surface without rocking. However, three legs are not as stable as four, so some caution must be observed when moving or leaning on this type of table. Splaying the legs more than those shown at the right would help. When the stools are not in use they can be pushed under the table, completely out of the way of passing traffic.

This is an end table made of formed plywood, veneered with hickory. There is nothing fancy about this table except the shape, but I like it because it is unique. The storage area has a closed-in feeling, but the top is open and roomy. It is somewhat heavy and difficult to move, but the casters solve that problem.

PHOTO AT LEFT George Nakashima was a furniture maker who loved using wood that looked as though it was just cut from the tree. This is a well-designed table in the style of Nakashima. A single slab of cherry forms the top, which has been thickness planed, sanded and finished. The base creates a nice contrast to the organic top, with precisely machined parts that fit together in crisp joints. A very nice example of cherry wood used in all its glory!

ABOVE PHOTO One of the features of this country dining table is the drawer storage. Place mats, silverware, even board games are all easily accessible.

One of the unique and outstanding features of this conference table is the sunburst veneer pattern on the top. Cutting a 3" bullnose on the edge of the top, using cherry veneer that will age to a warm patina, and rounding the ends all serve to make this an inviting conference table.

Pine is usually associated with plain country furniture. This elegant little end table uses pine wood, with all its knots, to make a different statement. Putting a profile on the legs and adding raised panels to the box breaks up the straight lines. One added feature is that the top opens revealing plenty of storage for extra magazines and books. A remote control for the television could also be hidden in here if necessary!

The shape of this lamp table is fairly simple, and the decoration of its basic shape is a lot of fun. The proportions are just right. The base isn't too heavy, but it has enough mass to hold the table steady, and the top is made lighter by the tapestry look of the apron. The bamboo motif around the edge of the top complements the reedlike curved legs. This is a good example of how paint can help enhance the shape of the individual elements that make up a piece of furniture. The lighter color also helps these elements create their own shadows and highlights.

The shape of this table is unique, as are the legs and the carved panel sides. Every part of this table has something to say. It is a very busy piece, yet all the elements work together well. The wood is dark, which hides the carving somewhat until you get closer. The curving legs and scrollwork at the bottom of the panels serve to lighten the look of this piece. It could look boxy if the legs were straighter or not as long, and if the panels were straight across their bottoms.

This is called the Three Diamond coffee table. The painted top simplifies its shape, and your eye is more easily drawn to the glass as a result. The natural color of the red oak base is complemented by the color of the paint chosen for the top. Also note the clipped corners on the top, which soften the look and feel of the table.

This coffee table has a one-board maple top that was chosen for its unique grain coloring. It was then crosscut and matched to itself. The resulting two pieces were left separated from one another. The base is made of cherry. The staggered side and end aprons permitted longer tenons to be used to connect the legs without the tenons interfering with each other. The side aprons are held higher than the tops of the legs, giving the top a floating look. The legs flare slightly, which gives the table a solid visual connection with the floor.

chairs, stools and rockers

The rocker at the right was copied from a photo of a Limbert rocker with inlays in the legs. It is comfortable and will seat one adult and one child easily. To simplify the construction of this chair, the same bending form was used to fabricate the rockers, the crest rail and the front radius on the arms. The arched side and front and back seat rails lighten the look of the chair and add some movement.

When you sit, you might as well sit in **comfort** and **style**.

This bench is made in the Greene and Greene style. The basic shape of the bench is simple, yet it is a unique design. The slight jog in the upper front leg, the slight flaring of the back at its sides, the wonderful shapes of the back slats, the shape of the arms and the pegged joinery make this piece what it is.

I know a lot of furniture makers who won't build chairs. Chairs can be tricky because they need to be sturdy, yet look nice. The joinery needs to be strong and unyielding.

The other part of chairmaking, probably the most difficult, is designing. It is my opinion that chairmaking can be the culmination of a cabinetmaker's talents.

Chairs are mostly air and take up space that doesn't have anything in it. A good chair design involves stress analysis, reading the grain in wood and using it properly, creating bullet-proof joinery and a design that says, "Come, sit and be comfortable."

Many times a great-looking chair is terribly uncomfortable to sit in. In certain instances it is permissible to use a chair only as decoration, but my practical side and my years of working in cabinet and furniture shops make me want to combine the best of all things — good design and solid construction yielding a usable and comfortable chair. As with any furniture project, once the basic dimensions have been decided, the real work of designing the piece begins.

Chairs can be made from any type of wood. The way the grain is used is what's important. Any joint needs to have wood grain that is free from curl, knots or other imperfections. However, these imperfections can become perfections in other places on the chair!

a BASIC CHAIR

My first chair is still standing proud! It's about as basic and no-nonsense as I could make it: four legs, a back and a seat.

THE FIRST CHAIR I EVER BUILT was made of clear grained maple. It had four legs, two side rungs, a back top rail, four rails for the seat, four corner blocks to strengthen the seat rail-to-leg joints and a seat. I used two dowels at each joint of the legs, rungs and seat rails. The back top rail had a curve, and the seat was scooped out just a little.

This chair, at right, is still in use and none of the joinery has loosened in the slightest. It has withstood the abuse of my son and two daughters! My point here is that with careful planning and building, it is possible to make a sturdy chair that will last. I believe that the combination of the doweled joinery and the hard maple has been the secret to the longevity of this chair.

The side rungs are placed about 8" off of the floor in this particular chair. This is a good height for rungs on a chair with straight legs. If they are located lower, the chair would look a little squatty. Using only 1½" material for the legs and all the rails also gives the chair a visually lighter look.

The legs are held firmly in place with the rungs and the seat rails. The combination of a rung, seat rail, front leg and rear leg makes up a side. Think of it as a cabinet with two sides, with face-frame rails holding those two sides together. The back rail is wider and adds a lot of lateral strength. The seat is simply screwed into place through oversized holes in the seat rails to allow for the seasonal movement of the solid-wood seat. This seems to have worked because the seat is still solid — no cracks!

For an even lighter visual look, the rungs could have been eliminated, but the structure of the chair would have been greatly compromised. In that case, the side seat rails would have had to bear the stress of a person leaning against the back. The joint at the back leg and the seat rail would have failed quickly.

A lot of chairs are made with no rungs. Queen Anne-style chairs are probably the most common of this type. These chairs look elegant and formal, and have been made for a couple of hundred years in the same style. I have repaired my share of them over the years, as have most craftsmen that do furniture work. The chair will work well if it is not used regularly, but that is not usually the case. Corner blocks can be added for strength to the seat-rail and rear-leg joint, but eventually the joint will be stressed and fail.

So do we stop making Queen Anne chairs? No, we keep building them because they look so good! What we can do is rethink the joinery and the glues used to secure those joints. But the bottom line is, the joint is not bulletproof.

I recommend anyone interested in

With careful planning and building, it is possible
to make a sturdy chair that will last.

making chairs to start with a basic chair, then try different types of joinery, leg shapes, seat shapes, seat heights and widths and probably most important, back support. Try using even and odd numbers of spindles in chair backs and see how they feel. Do they put pressure in the wrong places, on the backbone, for example? You'll probably find that even numbers of spindles will work better because there is no middle spindle in the center of the back. Try different shapes of back support systems. Cut out the center of an otherwise solid back splat and see if that will reduce backbone stress.

Experiment with different seat-to-back angles. See what happens when the angle is too severe. Try to find the angle that eases you into the chair and cradles you. Try scooping out a wooden seat and see what that does for your seat comfort.

Play with all the different ways there are to make a leg —turned, carved, curved, straight and square.

Have fun!

PHOTO ABOVE This is a beautifully carved and painted chair — the back detail speaks for itself.

PHOTO AT LEFT Sometimes, just a simple stool is all that's needed. The seat is 12" in diameter, 18" high and very comfortable.

a TALL STOOL

LIKE MOST SELF-RESPECTING cabinetmakers, I have done some damage to my back over the years by lifting cabinets the wrong way, so I needed a stool with a back to support my back!

My furniture is sometimes the result of what I have available in the way of materials. In the case of this stool, I had some very nice 8/4 soft maple left over from a job, perfect for my stool legs and rungs. A couple of scraps of mahogany for the back top rail and seat added a nice contrast to the maple.

Once the overall dimensions were determined (about a 28" seat height and a comfortable 18"-wide by 18"-deep seat), I then set about the task of making something that would look good. I had clients who came into my shop, so I wanted something that was both functional and visually pleasing.

To break up the straight leg design, I decided to set the legs at a slight angle. All the legs come together at the top at about a 3° angle.

I wanted the stool to be strong, of course, so I made the rungs and seat rails 2" wide. I also chose to stagger the rungs at each leg so that there would be plenty of material in the legs to create the joinery.

The back rail is curved in one plane. This part was to support my aching back, so I made sure it would have some stress relief in the right places. The piece of mahogany for the rail has a dark mineral streak in it that forms an arch, so I incorporated that into the design. After the curve was cut across the streak, it seemed to smile at me and say that I had made a good choice. That dark mineral streak adds a little touch that makes this stool special. When you're designing furniture, look for the grain patterns and make them part of your designs.

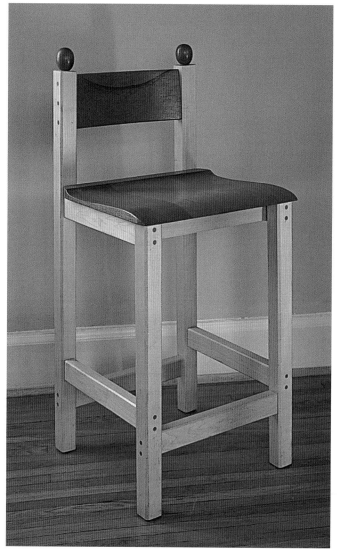

I chose to screw this stool together. Now before you say that I'm lazy, hear me out. I used 3" steel sheet-metal screws. The steel is strong and the threads on sheet-metal screws are close together, so the pulling power (or the mechanical advantage of a long tapering wedge, which is what a screw is) is great and thus the holding power is greatly increased. I predrilled holes and countersunk the screws 3/8" to allow room for mahogany plugs. To strengthen the joints even more, I dipped the screws in glue before screwing them into place.

I have used this chair for years now, and it is still as solid as on the day I built it. By carefully measuring where I located the screws, I was able to create a nice visual pattern on the legs.

I've learned that even a slight scoop in a wooden seat adds a surprising amount of comfort for one's posterior. The scoop on the seat at the left is in one dimension only, but that was all I needed. The scoop is only about 1/2" deep but it lets you slide right into the seat and holds you there very comfortably.

The back legs ended rather abruptly at their tops, so I added the turned mahogany eggs to help ease the legs into a nice ending. They serve only to add a little fun to the overall feel of the stool.

When you're designing furniture, look for the grain patterns and make them part of your design.

The fun part of making this chair was the joinery — or lack thereof. By using butt joints and 3" steel screws, I made very strong joints. The mahogany plugs add a visual question: What's really behind those plugs?

The back piece of this stool is a scrap of mahogany that was in my stash pile. As it turns out, it had a smiley grain streak in it just waiting to be discovered.

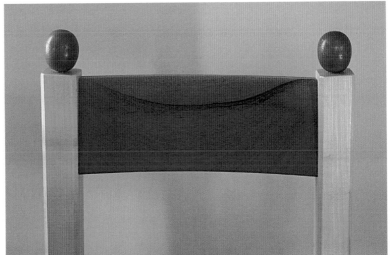

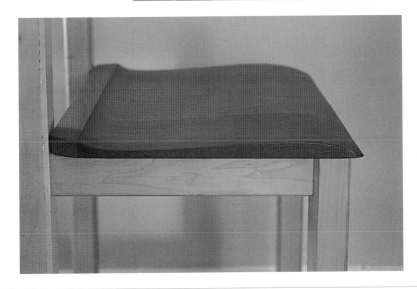

Scooping or shaping a wooden seat adds a surprising amount of comfort to a chair. It holds you in the chair, conforms to your body and creates an interesting design element.

a SHORT STOOL

WHEN WORKING AT THE BENCH for an extended length of time a woodworker's back can become stiff and sore. I decided to make myself a stool that would help remedy this situation. I wanted the stool to be just the right height for me to sit and work at eye level at my bench.

This stool below is 24" high and has a 14"-diameter seat with padding. That's a good-size seat for extended sitting. I wanted to be able to turn around and scoot across my shop to get a tool that was out of reach — mostly because it's fun to roll around the shop once in a while.

I like the graceful look of three-legged stools. They will also sit solidly on any uneven floor without rocking. But they can tip easily, so I decided that four feet were better than three in this case.

The rolling-around part was easy: I put casters on the ends of the legs. The legs are scrap 2×4 material I had in my wood racks. I wanted to keep the look of the stool solid but not clunky.

Remembering that stools occupy space, I decided to let some of that space show through the legs. They ended up being two angled frames interlocked at 90° to one another. This made a solid base.

The turning-around part took a little work. First, I mounted a round subtop on this base. Next I set a 2"-long

by ½"-diameter steel rod into the center of this subtop so that it protruded about ¾", and I set eight drawer roller glides into the subtop near its outer edge. Then I drilled the seat on its underside with a ½"-diameter hole in the center that fit over the protruding rod (see photo at right). When the seat was placed on the subtop it spun quite nicely! Four casters and some seat padding completed the stool. A coat of white paint gave it a nice, bright look. It really is very comfortable and has served its purpose well.

ABOVE PHOTO A steel pin, a hole in the bottom of the seat and some drawer rollers are all you need to make your own spinning seat.

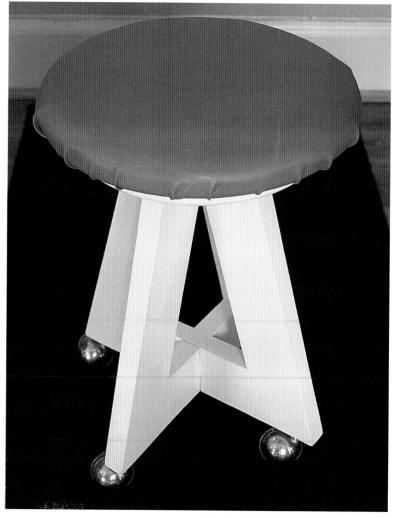

PHOTO AT LEFT Although nothing fancy, this stool is comfortable and practical.

You never know what might be in your backyard! Branch furniture is fun to make and offers some challenges of its own when it comes to creating a design. You are forced to work with the materials you have at hand, and no two pieces of furniture will be the same. The only specialized tool needed for this project was a tenon cutter that fits into an electric hand drill. (See suppliers list on page 127.)

This Celtic-looking chair is very basic — four legs, a seat and a back. It doesn't get much simpler than this. But the simplicity is balanced with the carved back and octagonal, tapered legs. The construction was actually fairly easy. A paper pattern was attached to a blank of wood to form the back, the holes were cut with a jigsaw, and the knots were given some depth by using a chisel to create relief points. The back has two tenons inserted into mortises in the seat. Likewise, the legs are attached to the seat with wedged tenons. This is a remarkably sturdy chair.

a DESK CHAIR

A JURIED WOODWORKING SHOW was coming up in my city, so I decided to build a chair and desk set. I was into curves at the time and wanted to explore that as a major design element. The chair shown at right is the result of that exploration.

This was a challenging piece to make. As I stated at the beginning of this chapter, chairs occupy space in a three-dimensional way. We can walk around chairs, pick them up and, of course, sit on them. I wanted to create a chair that had a seat that looked like it was floating, had good lumbar support and feet that looked like they were firmly planted on the floor.

With these criteria in mind, I sketched a lot of ideas on notepaper. When I started seeing on paper what I was seeing in my mind, I made a full-size sketch. It wasn't to scale and it wasn't final, but it gave me a good idea of what the chair was going to look like. I stood the drawing up against a table, which gave me a good sense of the proportions of the chair.

Then I created a full-scale plan complete with the leg curve patterns and the side rung patterns. This chair became a challenge when I realized that I wanted the front legs to be farther apart than the back legs. This small feature serves to complicate the construction techniques. Coupling that with the fact that I wanted the side rails to be curved, I had to visualize how this was going be done. I used some scrap wood to make mock-ups of how I wanted the joinery. By doing this I was able to balance my design with the practical business of making the chair.

The photo above shows how I decided to make the back support. First I made a pattern that matched the curve in my

I wanted a chair that looked as if it was solidly planted on the floor. I experimented with flared legs and this design succeeded — at least in my humble opinion. The curved legs create visual movement and the chair looks like it is growing out of the floor. I wanted the chair to invite you to sit down. The floating look of the seat is achieved by attaching the front legs in the middle of the seat. The curved slat that forms the back of this chair gives good lumbar support.

back, and then I made a bending form that matched this curve. The back splat is made of thin pieces of wood laminated together on this form. The top and bottom back rails hold this back splat in place, and it does a wonderful job of supporting one's back.

To give the top of the back legs some kind of conclusion, I simply curved the tops of the legs. I echoed this curve by putting a bullnose on the top edge of the top back rail.

One of the things that did not work well on this chair, however, is the seat. It is not deep enough to let a person slide back into the chair and relax his legs.

The chair is very sturdy because the front legs are almost in the middle of the seat, which helps to strengthen the joint

where the seat side rail meets the back leg. To add to the inviting look of the chair, I bullnosed the front and side seat rails and put a ¼" roundover on all edges of the legs and rungs. This softened the look and the feel of the chair.

As I said earlier, one of the things I wanted this chair to do was appear to be firmly sitting on the floor. I accomplished this by flaring the legs as they approach the floor. It seems as if the legs have feet that are reaching for the floor, which gives the chair a solid look. A measure of visual lightness is still kept by making the back splat thin and curving. The wood of choice for this project was mahogany because it darkens with age and acquires a beautiful, deep, red-orange patina.

ABOVE PHOTO Looking for one of the most comfortable chairs ever? This would be it. Big and roomy, strong and solid, this Arts & Crafts chair will last for generations and never go out of style. The front legs have a reverse stair-stepped look that widens as your eye follows the legs up from the floor. This leads to the arms, which are outspread, inviting you to sit down and relax. The angle of the back of the seat is perfect. Be careful sitting in this, though; you may not want to get up again!

ABOVE PHOTO Here's an idea a friend of mine had: Take your Arts & Crafts furniture outside. He built a morris chair out of treated lumber, painted it and took it out on the deck. What better way to relax and have that cold drink perched right at your fingertips?

My friend also made a replica of a *Titanic* deck chair. This elegant lounge chair was reproduced from information obtained on two surviving chairs from the great luxury liner *Titanic*. Not a wasted line in this design. It invites you to sit back and relax.

ROCKING CHAIRS

This rocker is wide and really comfortable. It is made to sit on the porch and help you rock your worries away. I wanted to have as few individual parts as possible on this chair, so the arms are also the front legs. Next time I might curve the arms and front legs right on under the chair, making them part of the rocker, too!

I made this bentwood rocker for my youngest daughter many years ago as a Christmas present. It required three different bending forms to create the front legs, back legs, rungs and seat slats. The seat, back slats and rungs are all notched to fit the legs. The seat height is 10".

ROCKING CHAIRS ARE ONE OF the greatest inventions known to man. After you spend some time in a rocking chair, your stress seems to just fade away.

The first rocker I made was for my three-year-old daughter (boy, was that a long time ago!). It was an experiment in lamination bending of wood strips. I wanted it to have a light look and also be physically light so she could carry it around with her if she wanted.

A rocker works by giving back some of your spent energy. All you have to do is lean back and give a little push with your legs. Children have enough energy to make this happen even if their feet don't touch the ground! They take to rockers

and rocking like no one else, knowing what to do and how to keep it going.

The action of a rocker can be further enhanced by turning the rockers in toward one another from front to back. Having the rockers slightly tilted towards each other in the back helps the rocker return to upright quicker, and keeps it in the same place so it doesn't slide sideways across the floor while you're rocking. This can happen if the rockers aren't perfectly parallel to each other or aren't slightly turned inward, trust me!

Rockers will outlive chairs with feet on the ground because there is less stress on the joints. They aren't subjected to being lifted or scooted across the floor, having a

person squirm around or (and this is the biggest killer of all chairs) being tipped back on the two back legs. This last provides enough stress on the joints to cause a chair to cry. When you sit in a rocker, the stress is transferred to the rockers, which takes that energy and causes you to lean back a little, thereby relieving your stress and a little of its own joint stress.

Glider chairs and benches work on the same principle of stress relief, but it be-

This rocker has a little of everything — turned legs, bent back rails, carved back spindles and solid-wood rockers cut to shape. This is a well-proportioned chair that just begs you to sit in it and rock.

comes more of a swinging motion, which is also very therapeutic.

Some of the early rockers were a combination of both rocker and glider, called platform rockers. They were made of a footed base with the rocker mounted on the base. To hold the rocking chair in place, springs were attached to both the base and the chair. This created an interesting rocking motion that felt a little like rocking and somewhat like gliding. The complete freedom of a full-blown rocker couldn't quite be achieved, but it was very comfortable indeed.

One other version still made today is the upholstered platform rocker which has been turned into a reclining chair that locks into place and becomes a bed of sorts. Talk about the perfect chair!

Smaller and larger radii on rockers can make a big difference in the rocking motion of the chair and should be experimented with by anyone interested in rocker "theory." A basic chair can be mocked up and different rockers applied to the legs of the chair. Test-drive these and see what you can come up with.

The Shakers made custom chairs to fit each individual in the community. When various events were held and seating was needed, everyone would bring their own chair. Rockers weren't necessarily carried around, but they were made with the same care and great craftsmanship as was all Shaker furniture. The rocker shown in this photo has features that make the simple design very interesting: The short rockers make it possible for the chair to be located in a small area. The woven seat and back have just the right amount of support and "give." The arms are fairly high up from the seat, giving the chair a cozy feeling when you sit in it. And the knobs on the ends of the front legs help keep the arms tight to the legs.

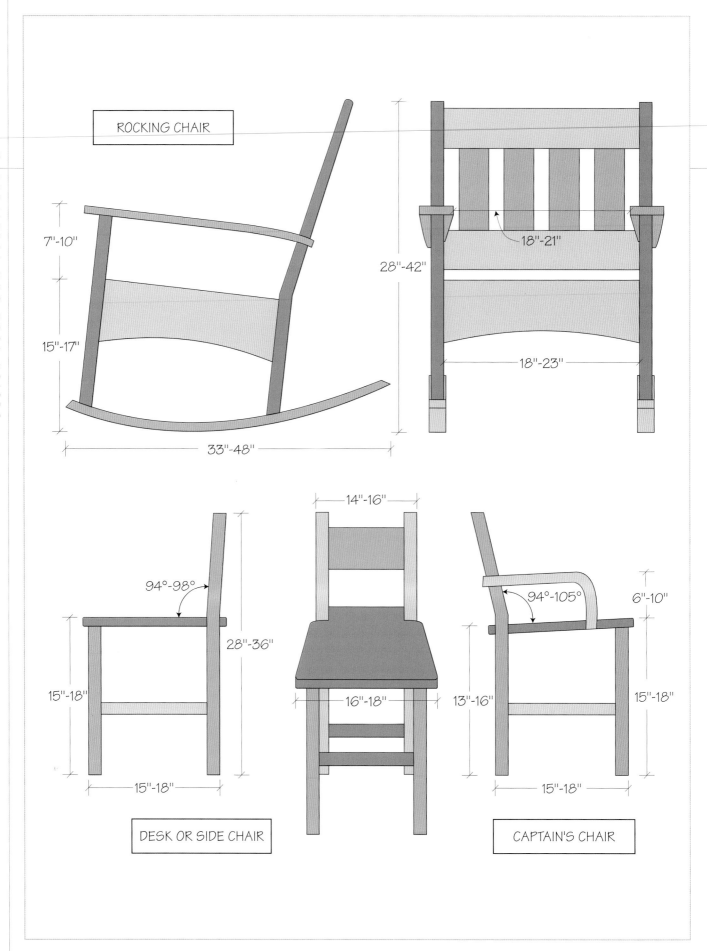

ROCKING CHAIR

7"-10"

15"-17"

28"-42"

18"-21"

18"-23"

33"-48"

14"-16"

94°-98°

28"-36"

15"-18"

16"-18"

15"-18"

DESK OR SIDE CHAIR

94°-105°

6"-10"

13"-16"

15"-18"

15"-18"

CAPTAIN'S CHAIR

To make a custom chair, it's a good idea to make a mock-up of the chair and fit it to a particular person.

chair facts

- Stools range from a seat height of 17" to 30". A bar stool is 30" high at the seat. The typical bar height is 42". From the seat to the top of the bar, allow 12" for leg room.
- Rocking chair seat heights are 15" to 17", and the slope of the seat from front to back is 4° to 8° down from horizontal.
- Rocker radii are 30" to 40". Make a mock-up of the rocker and test it before making the permanent rockers.
- Armrests on a captain's chair should be 18" to 22" apart at the front of the chair and taper toward each other to the back of the chair.
- Lumbar support is crucial to the success of a comfortable chair and should start 7" to 11" above the seat as a curve in the back of the chair. Matching the curve of the spine is best.
- To make a custom chair, it's a good idea to make a mock-up of the chair and fit it to a particular person.

When it comes to sheer sitting comfort, this Eastwood-style chair is hard to beat. It has all the traditional Arts & Crafts features — mortise-and-tenon joints, quartersawn white oak wood that is a medium brown color and thick padded cushions for the ultimate in comfort. The Arts & Crafts-style looks simple, but little details make it work. The through-tenons at the tops of the front legs stand ⅛" proud of the top of the arm, and the arms have the front and back corners cut off, wrapping around the back legs, softening the look of the chair. The rungs are set close to the floor, which gives the chair a solid look.

wall and base cabinets

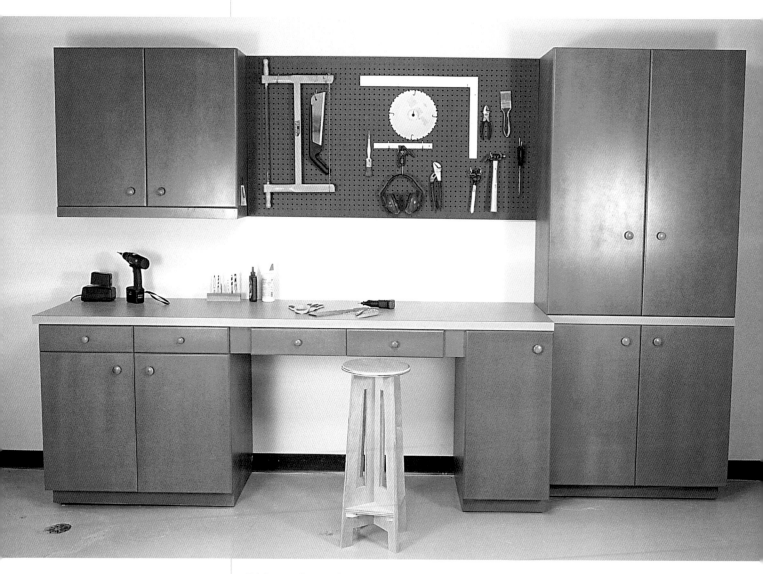

This is a set of practical cabinets that are made from medi-
um-density fiberboard (MDF) and finished with clear lacquer.
They use basic cabinet construction and can be arranged in
any configuration that is needed.

One of the most practical things you can build is a wall or **base cabinet.** The

design possibilities are almost endless — and it all starts with a basic box.

CABINETS

When I first started in the furniture-making and cabinetmaking business, I worked in a shop that built anything the clients wanted. But our main source of revenue was building cabinets — cabinets for kitchens, bathrooms, dens, closets, hospitals, restaurants, banks — the list seemed never-ending.

A cabinet is a box with doors, drawers (which are just little boxes inside bigger boxes) and pullout shelves. I liken cabinetmaking to Hollywood, because all of the focus is on the surface, but what is behind the finished piece is solid, hard work.

Most of the time, the cabinet boxes don't have to be works of art. They need to be sturdy and the right size and shape. Works of art are made by adding the doors, drawer fronts, false panels, face frames and mouldings.

When a woodworker is starting out, cabinetmaking is the best place to start learning. Once the basic techniques of cabinetmaking are learned, all other furniture making is easier.

The arrangements of base and wall cabinets are flexible. A kitchen is one specialized arrangement of cabinetry. The base cabinets serve as storage units and hold a worktop in place. The wall cabinets serve as storage units and can have lights mounted under them to illuminate the countertop. Also, if the wall cabinets don't finish out to the ceiling, their tops can be used to display things.

Cabinetry becomes part of a room. Kitchen and bathroom cabinetry is often attached to the walls, making it a perma-

A cabinet is a box with doors, drawers (which are just little boxes inside bigger boxes) and pullout shelves.

nent part of the house. Design elements that need to be considered when building cabinetry are the finish, types and styles of mouldings to be applied and how the piece will be used.

BASE CABINETS

When cabinetry is mentioned, kitchens are usually what comes to mind, so let's talk about them first.

When I was growing up, we spent a lot of time in the kitchen. It was a gathering place for the family, our friends and neighbors. Of course, food was prepared, but homework was done on the table, science projects were constructed and haircuts given, all in the kitchen.

In deciding how to arrange your kitchen, look at the room: Where are the windows and doors? What are the heights of the window sills? How high are the ceilings, and how much square footage does the room have? Do you cook a lot or do you mostly fix prepackaged meals? Do you want to have a table and chairs in the kitchen? Do you entertain a lot? Do you

have some special dishes you want to see on display? Do you like the look of wood, solid colors or laminate patterns (of which there are thousands)? All of these questions need to be asked and answered completely before anything else can be done.

The drawings on pages 104 and 105 show the basic dimensions and configurations of kitchen base and wall cabinets. If you use this information and nothing else, you won't go wrong. When designing, always start with the simplest idea first, then build on that.

Kitchen cabinets are built to certain standard dimensions (see "Kitchen and Bathroom Cabinet Facts" on page 109). Design your kitchen layout using these various cabinet sizes in combinations that will work in your kitchen space. It's easier to use and remember these standard sizes.

Sometimes, though, you just can't get standard-size cabinets to fit in the space you have. For example, the space between the walls, a door or a window is creating a problem. Use the standard cabinets where you can. Usually only one custom-size cabinet will be needed to fill in that space.

Base cabinets can have two pullout shelves (which I think are a great idea). One shelf is mounted at the bottom of the cabinet, and one is mounted halfway between the bottom of the cabinet and the bottom of the drawer at the top of the cabinet. Adjustable shelves, drawers,

This Shaker wall cabinet (5"-deep by 20"-wide by 28"-tall) is perfect for a small room. The depth will hold bottles, combs and other personal items. It is a straight-line cabinet with a couple of design elements that make it more than just a box with a door. The frame and panel door with the raised panel and the flat crown moulding make this cabinet a visual treat. The wood selection also makes a strong statement!

One simple but effective way to finish the top of a wall cabinet is to add crown moulding. The moulding adds a flair to the top, and it gives the cabinet depth as you look up at it. Dentil moulding underneath the crown can add even more flair.

This is a detail photo of a face-frame mounted hinge. These hinges are adjustable up and down but not in and out or sideways. This is an overlay door that is cut to fit over the cabinet, opening a certain distance all around, so little or no adjustment is necessary.

turntables for a lazy Susan and trash can holders can also be added to base cabinets.

Kitchen appliances mounted under kitchen cabinets are made to standard sizes. (See "Kitchen and Bathroom Cabinet Facts" page 109.) Of course, there are exceptions, but you should have no trouble finding what you want.

I don't think there is such a thing as a traditional kitchen anymore. There are wood cabinets with raised- and flat-panel doors, crown moulding trim that is stained or painted, flat doors and drawer fronts with laminate or wood veneers that are stained or painted; I even built a base cabinet that had 20-gauge stainless steel applied to the doors.

Cabinets can be built with face frames or no frames and with doors and drawer fronts that are mounted flush to the fronts of the cabinets or overlay the fronts. (See the illustrations on pages 104 and 105.) There are more cabinet combinations than can be listed here.

It seems there is never enough storage room for your shop tools. This one-piece cabinet will hold a lot of tools! It's a cabinet with two sides, four fixed shelves, three adjustable shelves and a drawer equipped with a router-bit storage board. The doors are overlay and use European hinges. This is cabinetry at its most basic, but it still has style. Note the beaded hardwood edges attached around the doors' and drawer front edges. This is a good project to construct if you want to learn the basics and gain some valuable shop storage at the same time!

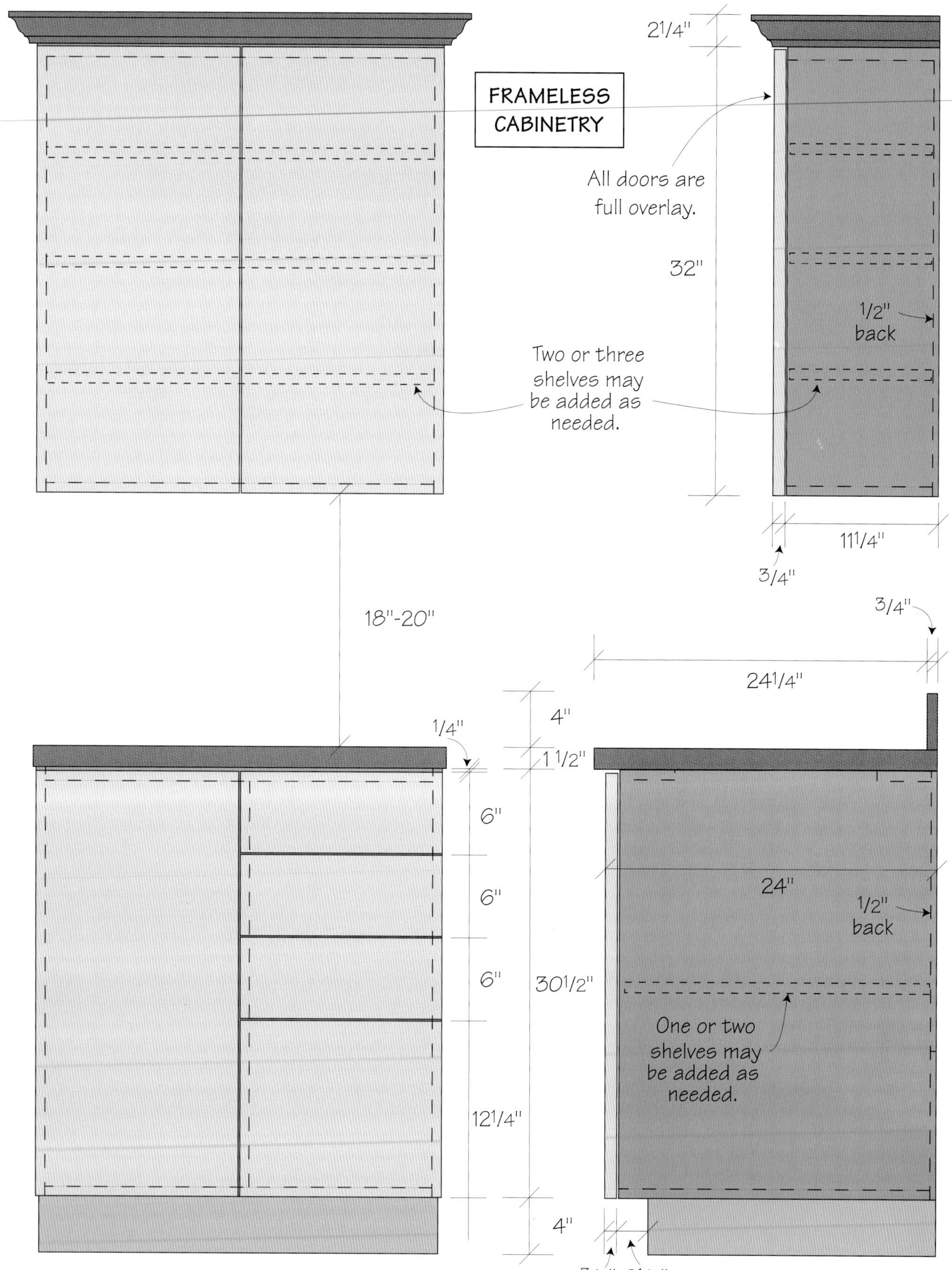

FRAMELESS CABINETRY

All doors are full overlay.

Two or three shelves may be added as needed.

$2^{1}/4"$

32"

$1/2"$ back

$11^{1}/4"$

$3/4"$

18"-20"

$3/4"$

$24^{1}/4"$

$1/4"$

4"

$1^{1}/2"$

6"

6"

6"

$30^{1}/2"$

$12^{1}/4"$

24"

$1/2"$ back

One or two shelves may be added as needed.

4"

$3/4"$ $2^{1}/4"$

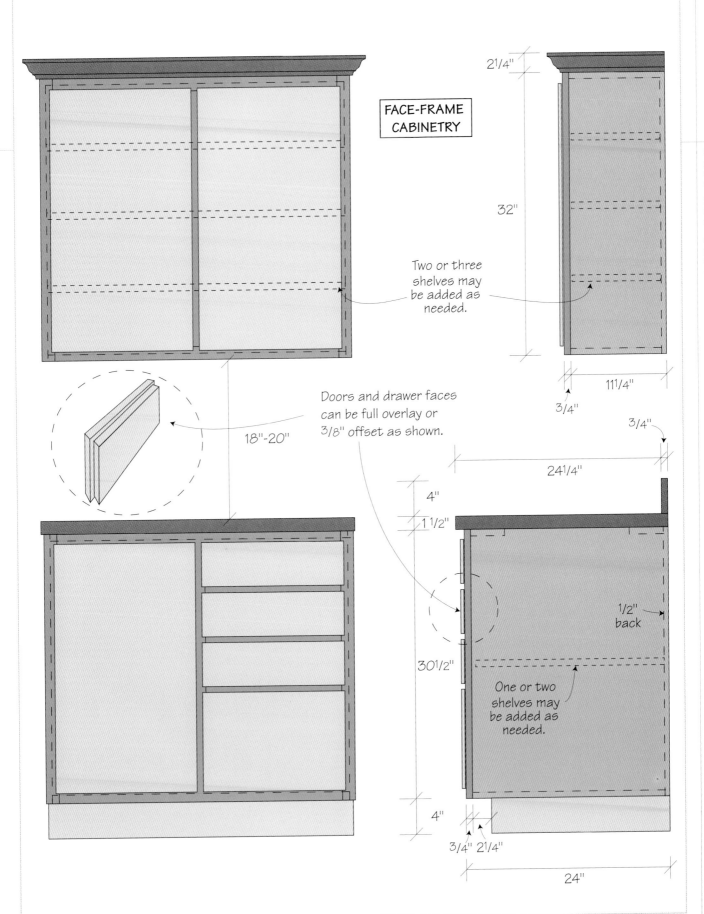

FACE-FRAME
CABINETRY

2¼"

32"

Two or three
shelves may
be added as
needed.

11¼"

¾"

Doors and drawer faces
can be full overlay or
3/8" offset as shown.

18"-20"

¾"

24¼"

4"

1½"

½"
back

30½"

One or two
shelves may
be added as
needed.

4"

¾" 2¼"

24"

the european or 32mm cabinetmaking system

For several decades, European cabinetmakers have used a system of cabinetmaking that is quick, flexible and efficient.

The cabinet parts are cut out, edge-banded, drilled as needed for hardware and finished. Then the drawer hardware and hinge plates are installed. One of the benefits of this system is that the cabinet parts can be shipped flat and delivered to the job site. The cabinets can then be assembled and installed.

It's called the 32mm system because the 5mm hardware mounting holes are drilled in a line 32mm on center. Two vertical rows of these 5mm holes are drilled on the inside of the cabinet side panels. The side panels have 8mm assembly holes drilled near the top and bottom edges. Matching 8mm holes are drilled into the edges of the bottom and top panels. The drawer boxes are predrilled for dowels or assembly screws.

All the necessary hardware for this construction system can be found at home improvement centers. The door hinges come in two parts: the hinge and its mounting plate. The drawer slides also come in two parts: the main part of the slide, which is mounted on the inside of the cabinet, and the drawer box part, which is mounted on the drawer. Special, deep-thread comfirmat assembly screws are used to hold the cabinets together.

Adjustable leveling feet can be mounted on the bottom of the cabinet. These are used to level the cabinets when they are installed and are adjusted with a screwdriver from the inside of the cabinet through a small hole drilled in the bottom of the cabinet. After the cabinets have been leveled and set, these holes are plugged with plastic covers. The feet also have clips that will accept cleats mounted on the cabinet base fronts. The base is simply pushed and clipped into place after the cabinets have been installed.

Hardware is available for hanging and leveling the wall cabinets. A hanger rail is attached level on the wall, cleats are attached to the back of the wall cabinet and then the cabinet is hung by these cleats on the rail. If front-to-back or end-to-end leveling is needed, access holes drilled in the back of the cabinet allow adjustment of the hanging cleats with a screwdriver. These holes are then plugged with a plastic cover.

Face frames are sometimes used with the European system. The frames can be built and finished separately, then put on the cabinets at final assembly. They are attached with glue and dowels or biscuits.

The drawer-box face panels have 25mm-diameter by 13mm-deep holes drilled into their backs to accept adjustable hardware used to mount the drawer faces to the drawer boxes. A machine screw is inserted into this hardware through the drawer-box front. After the drawers are put into the cabinet, these screws are snugged up and the drawer faces can be adjusted as needed. When all adjustments have been completed, permanent screws are added to hold the faces in place.

The cabinet doors are drilled with 35mm-diameter by 13mm-deep holes for the hinges. The hinges are pressed or set into place with two screws. After the cabinets have been installed, the doors are hung by clipping the hinges into place on the hinge plates. The door hinges can be adjusted with a screwdriver to line up the doors on the cabinets.

The backs of the cabinets are attached with screws, nails or staples driven into rabbets in the back edges of the side panels. The sides, bottoms, tops, shelves, bases, top rails

This is a typical self-closing European hinge. The hinge clips onto the plate, and the door can be removed without removing the hinge. A 35mm drill bit is used to cut the hole for the European hinges (photo on page 106).

(used on the base cabinets), doors and drawer-box front panels are $3/4$" or 19mm thick. The back panels, drawer-box sides, fronts, backs and bottoms are $1/2$" or 13mm thick. Sometimes $1/4$"- or 6mm-thick material is used for drawer bottom panels.

Countertops are $1^1/2$" or 38mm thick and 25" or 635mm deep and as long as necessary! Countertops can be made of butcher block, particleboard or plywood covered with high-pressure laminate, solid-surface materials, marble, colored concrete, ceramic tile set onto a plywood top or stainless steel.

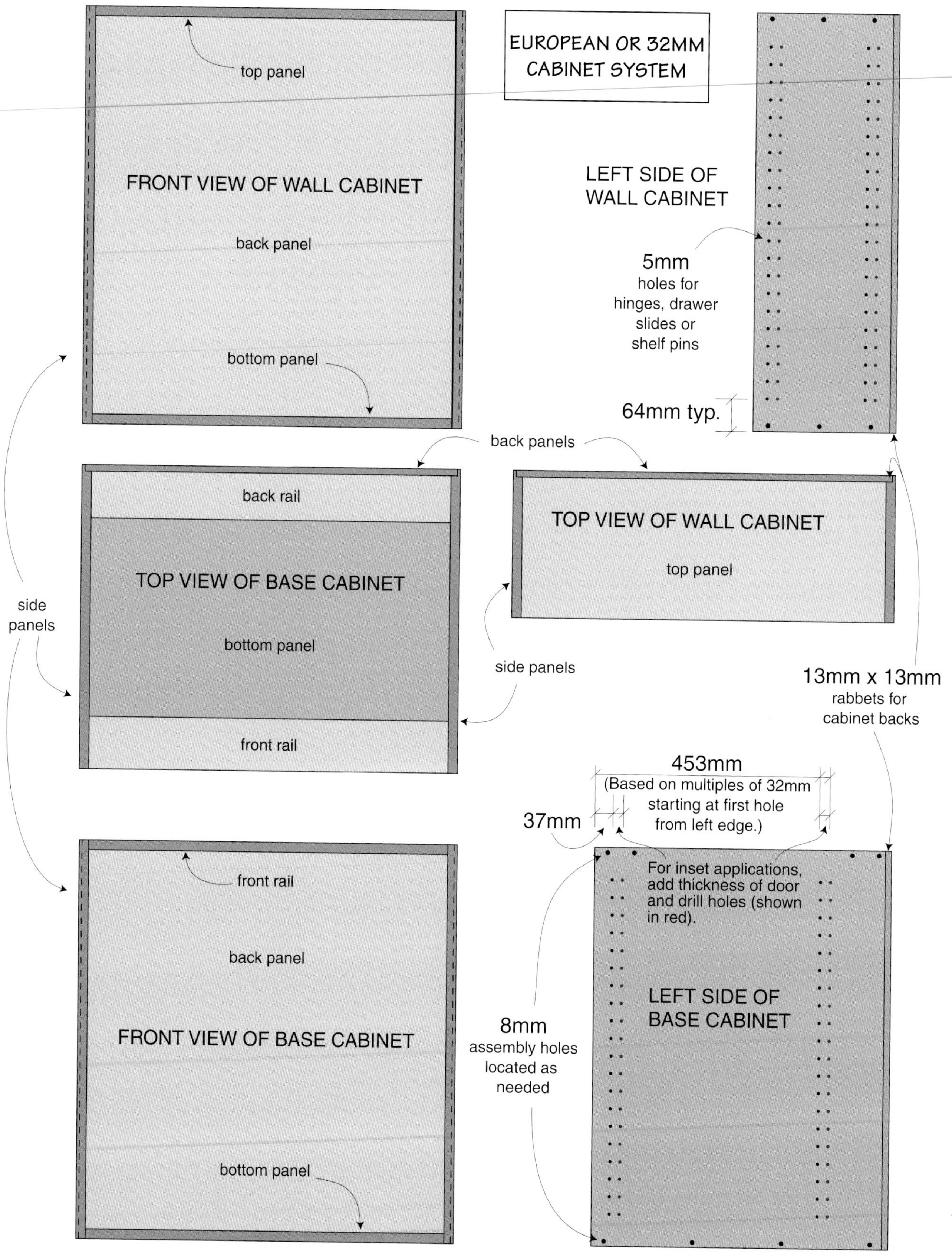

FRONT VIEW OF WALL CABINET

top panel

back panel

bottom panel

EUROPEAN OR 32MM
CABINET SYSTEM

LEFT SIDE OF
WALL CABINET

5mm
holes for
hinges, drawer
slides or
shelf pins

64mm typ.

back panels

TOP VIEW OF BASE CABINET

back rail

bottom panel

front rail

side
panels

side panels

TOP VIEW OF WALL CABINET

top panel

13mm x 13mm
rabbets for
cabinet backs

FRONT VIEW OF BASE CABINET

front rail

back panel

bottom panel

453mm
(Based on multiples of 32mm
starting at first hole
from left edge.)

37mm

For inset applications,
add thickness of door
and drill holes (shown
in red).

LEFT SIDE OF
BASE CABINET

8mm
assembly holes
located as
needed

ABOVE PHOTO This detail is at the top of the kitchen cabinets. By adding dentil moulding and crown moulding, the look of these flat-topped cabinets was simply, but dramatically, changed.

kitchen and bathroom cabinet facts

- Kitchen base cabinets are 12", 15", 18", 24", 30" and 36" wide.
- All kitchen base cabinets are built to finish 34½" high. This includes the base, which is 4" high. Most appliances are made with 4"-high bases.
- If you want to have cabinets that have a different base height and you are installing appliances, make sure the appliances will fit this new base height.
- If you choose to install custom or special-order appliances, check the base heights on these appliances. Some of them are not 4" high. You need to know this before you build all of your cabinets with 4" bases!
- Kitchen wall cabinets are made to the same standard widths as base cabinets.
- The heights of wall cabinets are 24", 30", 32", 36" and 42".
- Bathroom cabinets are 32" to 36" high.

PHOTO AT LEFT This is a typical kitchen cabinet setup. The base cabinet top is a little more shallow than normal to allow the small shelf to be installed at the back of the top.

This simple, fun, inexpensive and practical shelving for the bathroom has style, flair and a towel rack. What more could you ask for from a storage shelf? The crescent cutouts add that special touch, as does the scrollwork on the top, bottom and sides.

BATHROOM CABINETS

Bathrooms and kitchens have been the focus of home improvements for several years. Upgrading or redesigning these rooms increases the value of a home substantially.

Bathroom cabinets serve the same function as kitchen cabinets: Items are stored in the cabinets, and they support a work surface.

Traditionally, bathroom base cabinets are shorter than kitchen cabinets. The average height of a bathroom sink base is 32". I once built some bathroom cabinets that were 36" high because the clients were very tall. This was a great idea, because bending over to wash your face and brush your teeth seems silly when you could just walk up to the counter and be at a better height.

Wall cabinets in bathrooms can be 18" to 42" high. The amount of space in bathrooms can vary a lot, so using the space to its best advantage becomes the challenge. Many times, a closet or towel storage cabinet is built into a bathroom. These cabinets can be a wall cabinet, base cabinet or a combination that is built as one unit. A floor-to-ceiling cabinet can hold a lot of towels, first-aid materials and personal hygiene products.

Cabinets with doors and shelves are usually chosen so that the depth of the cabinets is shallow enough to allow storage without losing items that might get pushed to the back of the cabinet. A common size is 12" to 20" deep. Drawers can be installed in the deeper cabinets (starting at 18" deep).

Cabinets in bathrooms can be made of any material, but the finishes need to be impervious to water and high humidity. Many times, high-pressure laminate is chosen because of its tremendous durability. It can also be cleaned easily. With all of the styles, colors, patterns and textures available, laminate is a wise choice for bathroom cabinetry.

European hinges (see page 106) are used almost exclusively in bathroom cabinetry because of the wide range of door configurations that can occur in a bathroom. Windows, showers and lighting all enter the picture. Will the doors be full overlay? Do the cabinets fit against a wall or walls on the sides? Is there room for the doors to open past 90°? Is there enough room for the doors to open at least 90°, as this makes it easier to access the inside of the cabinet? The European hinges can be inset, overlay, swing from 90° to 270°, be mounted with the hinged edge of the doors $\frac{1}{8}$" from the wall and configured to hang doors on cabinets with angled faces.

One part of designing cabinets is deciding what style of handles and pulls to use on the doors and drawers. When I built kitchen and bathroom cabinets for clients, I told them to wait until the cabinets were installed before deciding what hardware to use. I discovered that many times, if the clients decided on the hardware and purchased it beforehand, they would change their minds and want to use different hardware after the cabinets had been installed.

The style, color and location of the hardware on the cabinets can make or break the feel and look of the whole project. Many times, this hardware decision can take days, but it is important to take your time, choose what you like and decide what fits best in the room.

Do the doors look better with knobs or handles? Should you use knobs on the doors and handles on the drawers? Is there enough room for the handles or knobs to allow the doors to open against a wall without hitting the wall? Should flush-mounted hardware (handles set into a recess routed into the door or drawer front) be used? Should any knobs or handles be used at all? Finger grooves can be routed into the bottoms of drawer fronts and the tops, bottoms or sides of doors. Touch-latch hardware is available that allows you to push on the door to open it. The possibilities are endless!

This Shaker wall cabinet has crown moulding at the top and crisp and stylish scrollwork at the bottoms of the sides. It was adapted to be screwed to the wall, rather than hung on a peg, but the style is the same. The choice of bird's-eye maple makes this cabinet unique.

This well-constructed wall shelving is made in the craftsman style. It has through-tenons and pinned joinery. The curves at the top and bottom of the sides and the bottom rail all complement each other. The beveled edges have a nice softening effect on the whole cabinet.

This is a somewhat rare cabinet that is based on a Byrdcliffe wall cabinet from the Arts & Crafts era. The painted relief carving on the door is whimsical and adds to the uniqueness of the cabinet. The door with the knob at the top and the uneven spacing of the shelf openings add a good balance and rhythm to this unit.

PHOTO AT LEFT This cabinet has a lot of features that work together to create a great display cabinet. The room had a niche that needed a special piece of furniture in it, and the clients have a unique collection of martini shakers that needed a place to be displayed. The three arched doors, the lights inside each section of the cabinet, fluted stiles that terminate into rosette blocks, the glass shelves and cherry stain are all combined in a way that make this piece work well. With the addition of the drawers at the bottom, the information papers for the martini shakers can be kept close at hand. The legs and top mouldings were kept simple so they didn't compete with the main part of the display case. The cabinet is made of alder, a nice but inexpensive wood, and stained a cherry color.

PHOTO AT RIGHT The Shaker storage cabinet here is plain and symmetrical. The square door panel and the square face of the cabinet work together to make this a solid unit. The painted base and natural wood top and knobs offer a nice contrast to one another. This cabinet looks better in a naturally lit room as shown here, rather than in a darker room where the painted cabinet could appear too large.

Wall-mounted cabinets aren't located only in kitchens or bathrooms. This cabinet and buffet are in a dining room. The wall cabinet serves as a display case for dishes and other items. These two pieces were originally going to be a one-piece buffet, but the separation of the units looks better and opens up the top of the buffet so it can be used as needed. The buffet might also be located in another part of the room on occasion.

chapter **12**

desks

I built the mahogany desk above for my father-in-law. He wanted it to be somewhat formal and elegant, practical and not too big. It's about 30" deep and 60" long. I made it in five parts — two drawer stacks, a pencil drawer, a front panel and a top. The glass top was added to preserve the veneered top.

Write that novel, do your homework, keep your personal records organized,

conduct business or sit with your feet up. Desks are a **unique** piece

of furniture that give us **privacy** and a place to do our best thinking.

This client wanted a desk that created a little privacy but would still have an open feeling. It is supported by two ⅓ cylinder legs and one gently curved leg. The legs echo the shape of the top and provide almost limitless leg, knee and chair room. The room had windows on two walls and was fairly large, so the 8'-long, dark walnut desk worked well in the space. One other advantage of making this desk of walnut was that it would change color quickly and acquire a rich reddish-brown patina. My client wanted this color at the beginning of the project, but I convinced him he would like the aged color better and would have it in three months. He called me a few months later to say the desk had turned color just like I had told him it would, and that it had been fun to watch the color change week to week!

Desks are special pieces of furniture that serve an important function as communication centers in our lives. We pay our bills, write letters, do homework, write books and journals, read or just sit and think at our desks. Desks can be conference tables or a place where two people can sit and chat.

When designing a desk, it's important to know where it will be located and how it will be used. Will you be spending a lot of time at the desk or just a few minutes at a sitting? Do you want natural light or will artificial lighting work? Do you need additional storage for reference books or other files?

In an office setting, a desk might need to be formal or function as a conference table. At home, it could be small and tucked away in a quiet corner, or be built into the kitchen and used as a communications center for the whole household.

This desk has a top, two drawer pedestals, a pencil drawer and a modesty panel between the pedestals. It can be taken apart into these basic components and moved easily. The base trim repeats the bevel and quirk detail on the top's edge. This is about as basic as this type of desk can be, but it has a character all its own.

The beveled top edge and quirk on this desk are easy to make, but they add interest to what could have been a plain desktop. After the desk was finished, the owner decided to have a piece of glass made to cover the top. The beauty of the mahogany shows through and remains unmarred.

PHOTO AT LEFT Many people think and work better on their feet. This desk will let them do just that. The design is basic, but the small details make it interesting. The flared legs give visual movement. Note the extra tapered bevel on the outside corner of each leg. This adds to the tapered look and lightens the look of the fairly thick leg. The stringers are curved in two dimensions and are bull-nosed on both edges to make the desk look more inviting. Another visual dynamic is created by raising the back stringer slightly. This is a small thing, but it makes a lot of difference in the look of the desk.

ABOVE PHOTO The front of the stand-up desk has two drawers set back slightly from the face of the desk. It's amazing what this does to the look of the front of the desk. It is no longer plain or flat, and the shadow lines make it more interesting. Choosing fitted drawers rather than overlay drawers makes the framework, including the quirk detail, visible.

A quirk was cut into the bottom front of the aprons on the stand-up desk. This simple but effective design detail adds a shadow line that can serve to break up a plain apron.

A Shaker sewing desk can also be used as a writing desk. The absolutely gorgeous curly maple used here changes the character of the original desk, which was most likely made with pine or cherry. This desk makes a bold statement, but it remains somewhat subdued because of the simple lines of the cabinetry. If a highly figured wood was available, the Shakers may have used it on the drawer fronts only.

This simple but elegant little desk is made of walnut. The drawer fronts are veneered and have small mouldings applied to their fronts. This is an effective way to enhance the look of drawer fronts, doors and cabinet sides. The quirk detail in the upper leg gives definition to the upper and lower portions of the legs.

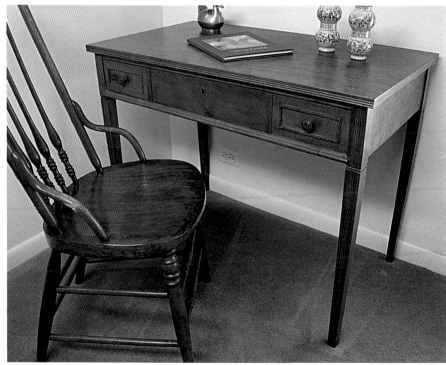

This desktop is a torsion box. Two spaces were created for the drawers before the whole top was glued up. When the drawers are closed, they blend into the bullnose on the rest of the desktop, creating a clean and undisturbed look. The bullnose was applied to the desk, then the drawer fronts were carefully cut out so the grain pattern on the fronts would match. The drawers were then made to fit their respective openings. The drawers are not to be seen until needed.

This desk is supported at three points, creating a very open and welcome look to those who enter this office. The client wanted to create a comfortable gathering around his desk for small group meetings by simply pulling up a few chairs. Each of the legs is wrapped in bookmatched walnut veneer that has a fairly straight grain. It was meant to contrast with the busy burled-veneer top and also to give a strong visual look. One other nice feature is that the legs are attached with cleats to the underside of the top. If the desk needs to be moved, the legs are simply removed for transport and reattached upon arrival.

PHOTO BELOW Mahogany wood changes with exposure to light. This desk and chair were made of mahogany with a clear finish. The wood aged to a warm reddish brown color that blends nicely into its surroundings. This desk has smooth lines, but those lines have a lot of movement. Sometimes, furniture like this is needed in simpler surroundings, but it doesn't have to be *simple* furniture. Subtle details can be powerful in the proper surroundings.

When you view this desk from either end, the legs appear to be standing on their own. Upon closer examination, however, you see that the legs are held in place by a stringer made of two laminated boards, curved at each of their ends. These boards are glued together and then doweled to the legs. It's a fun discovery to make when looking at the desk.

This secretary is based on the Chippendale style. This type of drop-front desk used to be very popular in a lot of homes. The shelving at the top kept reference books within reach; the drop front hides the important papers and can be locked; and the bottom has ample storage for just about anything! From a woodworker's point of view, this is a wonderful and challenging project to build.

ABOVE PHOTO This is a home office setup that is light, airy and efficient. The color of the painted bases may be chosen to match the room. This modular arrangement could be located in a corner or lined up against a wall. One advantage to having limited drawer space is that it forces you to keep only the most important papers and files!

PHOTO AT LEFT Computer workstations are one of the most popular pieces of home-office furniture. This particular piece is a neat way of having complete access to your computer equipment and being able to hide it when it's not being used. It has plenty of room for the monitor, speakers, keyboard, printer, scanner, paper and a few knick-knacks! Because it's made in sections (upper cabinet, base cabinet and top), it can be moved easily. All the materials for this cabinet are available at any home-improvement center.

The Burlington farmer's desk is a meeting of country and city. Made of pine and solid joinery, this practical desk can be closed to keep things private if necessary. It has cubbyholes for lots of storage, and because the sides are tall, it has a more private feel than having an open top. This is a good desk to sit at while writing letters.

This is a good example of how simple a desk can be. This Shaker trestle desk has two legs, a hidden stringer that connects them, a top and a drawer. It's small, which allows it to fit just about anywhere. The legs are distinctive and add a visual treat to an otherwise plain design. The incredible curly maple chosen for this desk sets it completely apart as one-of-a-kind.

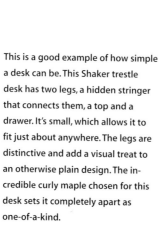

Explore a simple idea and new design ideas will come. This desk is made of laminated strips of wood put together in a clever way, and the result is very striking! The tempered glass top makes it possible to see all the action and detail of the base. This desk is about 3' wide and 5' long, but doesn't appear that large because the desk is mostly air and the glass top is almost invisible. It could work in a small room without being obtrusive.

This is a reproduction of a plantation desk. The use of pine makes this piece appear less formal than it could look. If it was made of cherry, walnut or figured maple, this desk would have a totally different look and feel. The upper cabinet is perfect to use as a bookcase. Other design options could include glass panel doors or no doors at all. The flip-top work surface has storage inside, and the small drawer can be accessed even if the desktop is being used. The legs are tapered only on the inside. This is an interesting way to open up the look of a table. They appear to reach outward from each other. If the legs are tapered on the outsides, they will appear to pull in toward each other. If the legs are tapered on all four sides, they will appear more delicate and graceful. These last two methods will also make the top of the table or desk appear heavier, so you will need to adjust the dimensions accordingly. As the legs are shown here, they will support more visual "weight" but still appear more graceful than straight legs.

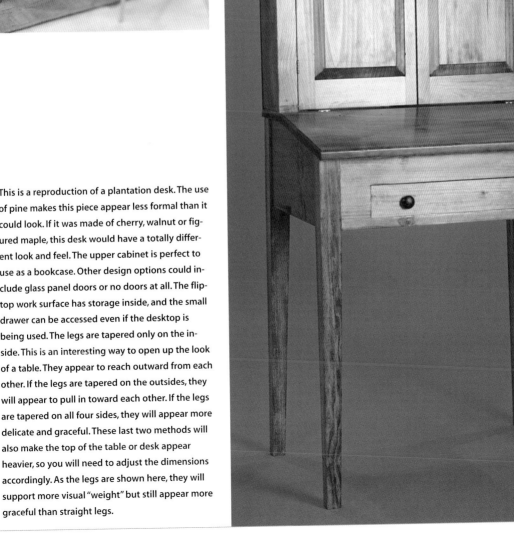

Today we use laptop computers, but Thomas Jefferson used a lap desk similar to this one. These were common a couple of hundred years ago and were used to store writing paper, bottles of ink, pens and letters. When riding in coaches or perhaps sitting outdoors, one would sit with this desk on one's lap to write correspondence. Nowadays, these are used as special-letter writing desks. They can also be used by artists to carry sketch paper, pencils, pastels and charcoal.

This is a handsome, small writing desk with cubbyholes and a top that can be folded down to hide the inside. It has several design elements that work together to create a classic piece. From the distinctively shaped and carved legs to the veneered fronts of the cubbyholes, the workmanship is outstanding. This is one of those desks where you would sit down to write a short letter or dash off some thank-you notes. Sit any longer and you would start to feel closed in and nonproductive. It is a nice piece of furniture that enhances the look of a room better than it functions as a working desk. That is not a bad thing, just something to consider when making a small desk like this.

A great writing desk can inspire great writing. This desk has the feel of a rolltop desk without the sliding tambour cover. When the table portion was finished, it was nice, but it needed more — a feeling of privacy. The upper cubbyhole and drawer section with the curved wraparounds were added, pulling this design together. The writing surface is faux leather and lifts up for additional storage. A lap or pencil drawer could have been installed in the front and would have worked well, also. Note the flared legs. This photo shows how these legs can give the table a feeling of being firmly rooted to the floor while holding up the top gracefully.

BEVEL A cut that is not 90° to a board's face, or the facet left by such a cut.

BISCUIT A thin, flat oval of compressed beech that is inserted between two pieces of wood into mating saw kerfs made by a biscuit or plate joining machine.

BRIDLE JOINT A joint that combines features of both lap joints and mortise and tenon. It has a U-shaped mortise in the end of the board.

BUTT JOINT Two flat facets of mating parts that fit flush together with no interlocking joinery.

CARPENTER'S GLUE White and yellow adhesives formulated for use with wood.

CASING The trim framing a window, door or other opening.

CHALK LINE Line made by snapping a chalk-coated string against a plane.

CHECK A crack in wood material caused by drying, either just in the surface or in the ends of the board so the fibers have separated.

COMPOUND MITER A cut where the blade path is not perpendicular to the wood's end or edge and the blade tilt is not 90° to the face.

COPING Sawing a negative profile in one piece to fit the positive profile of another, usually in moulding.

COUNTERBORE A straight-sided drilled hole that recesses a screw head below the wood surface so a wood plug can cover it, or the bit that makes this hole.

COUNTERSINK A cone-shaped drilled hole whose slope angle matches the underside of a flat screw head and sinks it flush with the wood surface, or the tool that makes this hole.

CROSSCUT To saw wood perpendicular to the grain.

CUPPING A drying defect where one side of the board shrinks more across the grain than the other, causing the board to curl in on itself like a trough.

DADO A flat-bottomed, U-shaped milling cut of varying widths and depths but always running across the grain.

DOVETAIL JOINT A traditional joint characterized by interlocking fingers and pockets shaped like its name. It has exceptional resistance to tension.

DOWEL A small cylinder of wood that is used to reinforce a wood joint.

DRESSING The process of turning rough lumber into a smooth board with flat, parallel faces and straight, parallel edges and whose edges are square to the face.

EDGE LAP A notch into the edge of a board halfway across its width which forms half of an edge lap joint.

FINGERLAP A specific joint of the lap family that has straight, interwoven fingers; also called a box joint.

FINISH Varnish, stain, paint or any mixture that protects a surface.

FLAT-SAWN The most common cut of lumber, where the growth rings run predominantly across the end of the board, or its characteristic grain pattern.

FLUSH Level with an adjoining surface.

GRAIN PATTERN The visual appearance of wood grain. Types of grain pattern include flat, straight, curly, quilted, rowed, mottled, crotch, cathedral, beeswing or bird's-eye.

HARDWOOD Wood from broadleaf deciduous trees, no matter what the density (balsa is a hardwood).

HEARTWOOD Wood from the core of a tree, usually darker and harder than newer wood.

JIG A shop-made or aftermarket device that assists in positioning and steadying the wood or tools.

JOINTING The process of making a board face straight and flat or an edge straight, whether by hand or machine.

KERF The visible path of subtracted wood left by a saw blade.

KEY An inserted joint-locking device, usually made of wood.

KNOCKDOWN JOINT A joint which is assembled without glue and can be disassembled and re-assembled if necessary.

LAP JOINT A type of joint made by removing half the thickness or width of the parts and lapping them over each other.

LENGTH JOINT A joint which makes one longer wood unit out of two shorter ones by joining them end to end.

LEVEL Absolutely horizontal.

MILLING The process of removing material to leave a desired positive or negative profile in the wood.

MITER A generic term meaning mainly an angled cut across the face grain, or specifically a 45° cut across the face, end grain, or along the grain. See also **BEVEL**.

MORTISE The commonly rectangular or round pocket into which a mating tenon is inserted. Mortises can be blind (stop inside the wood thickness), through, or open on one end.

PARTICLEBOARD A panel made of wood particles and glue.

PILOT HOLE A small, drilled hole used as a guide and pressure relief for screw insertion, or to locate additional drilling work like countersinking and counterboring.

PLYWOOD Panel made by laminating layers of wood.

QUARTERSAWN A stable lumber cut where the growth rings on the board's end run more vertically across the end than horizontal, and the grain on the face looks straight; also called straight-grained or riftsawn.

RABBET A milled cut which leaves a flat step parallel to, but recessed from, the wood's surface.

RAIL The name of the horizontal parts of a door frame.

RIP To cut parallel to the grain of a board.

SAPWOOD The new wood in a tree, located between the core (heartwood) and bark. Usually lighter in color.

SCARF JOINT A joint that increases the overall length of wood by joining two pieces at their ends, commonly by gluing together two unusually long bevels in their faces or edges.

SCRIBE To make layout lines or index marks using a knife or awl.

SHOULDER The perpendicular face of a step cut, like a rabbet, which bears against a mating joint part to stabilize the joint.

SOFTWOOD Wood from coniferous evergreen trees, no matter what the density (yew is a softwood).

SPLINE A flat, thin strip of wood that fits into mating grooves between two parts to reinforce the joint between them.

STAIN A pigment or dye used to color wood through saturation, or a discoloration in wood from fungus or chemicals.

STILE The name of the vertical parts of a door frame.

TENON The male part of a mortise-and-tenon joint, commonly rectangular or round, but not restricted to those shapes.

TONGUE AND GROOVE Joinery method in which one board is cut with a protruding groove and another is cut with a matching groove along its edge.

TWISTING A drying defect in lumber that causes it to twist so the faces at the end of the board are in a different plane.

VENEER A thin sheet of wood bonded to another material.

WIDTH JOINT A joint that makes a unit of the parts by joining them edge-to-edge to increase the overall width of wood.

SUPPLIERS

BALL AND BALL
463 West Lincoln Highway
Exton, PA 19341
800-257-3711
www.ballandball-us.com
Hardware reproductions.

CONSTANTINES WOOD CENTER
1040 E. Oakland Park Blvd.
Ft. Lauderdale, FL 33334
954-561-1716
www.constantines.com
Tools, woods, veneers and hardware.

THE HOME DEPOT
2455 Paces Ferry Road
Atlanta, GA 30339
770-433-8211
www.homedepot.com
Tools, paint, wood, electrical, garden.

HORTON BRASSES INC.
Nooks Hill Road
PO Box 95
Cromwell, CT 06416
800-754-9127
www.horton-brasses.com
*Hardware for antique furniture; Hepplewhite,
Chippendale and Victorian brass hardware;
hand-forged iron hardware.*

LEE VALLEY TOOLS LTD.
USA:
P.O. Box 1780
Ogdensberg, NY 13669-6780
800-267-8735
CANADA:
P.O. Box 6295, Station J
Ottawa, ON K2A 1T4
800-267-8761
www.leevalley.com
*Fine woodworking tools and hardware; design
and manufacture many quality tools under the
Veritas label.*

LOWE'S HOME IMPROVEMENT WAREHOUSE
1605 Curtis Bridge Road
Wilkesboro, NC 28697
800-890-5932
www.lowes.com
Tools, paint, wood, electrical, garden.

PAXTON WOODCRAFTERS' STORE
www.paxton-woodsource.com
*Domestic and foreign hardwoods; veneers;
books and woodworking tools.*

ROCKLER WOODWORKING AND HARDWARE
4365 Willow Drive
Medina, MN 55340
800-279-4441
www.rockler.com
Woodworking tools and hardware.

TOOL CRIB OF THE NORTH
1705 13th Ave., North
Grand Forks, ND 58203
800-358-3096
www.toolcribofthenorth.com
Discount mail order power tools.

VAN DYKE'S RESTORERS
P.O. Box 278
39771 S.D. HWY. 34
Woonsocket, SD 57385
800-558-1234
www.vandykes.com
*Supplies for upholstery and antique restora-
tion; antique reproduction hardware.*

WOLFCRAFT NORTH AMERICA
1222 W. Ardmore Ave., PO Box 687
Itasca, IL 60143
630-773-4777
www.wolfcraft.com
Woodworking hardware and accessories.

WOODCRAFT SUPPLY CORP.
560 Airport Industrial Park
P.O. Box 1686
Parkersburg, WV 26102-1686
(800) 225-1153
www.woodcraft.com
Woodworking hardware and accessories.

WOODWORKER'S SUPPLY
1108 North Glenn Road
Casper, WY 82601
800-645-9292
www.woodworker.com
*Woodworking tools and accessories, finishing
supplies, books and plans.*

INDEX